First edition for the United States, its territories and
dependencies, and Canada published in 2005 by Barron's
Educational Series, Inc.

Design: Balley Design Associates
Photography: Steve Tanner
Editor: Céline Hughes

All inquiries should be addressed to:
Barron's Educational Series, Inc.
250 Wireless Boulevard
Hauppauge, NY 11788
www.barronseduc.com

ISBN-13: 978-0-7641-3223-0
ISBN-10: 0-7641-3223-7

Library of Congress Catalog Card Number 2004116539

Printed in China
9 8 7 6 5 4 3 2 1

the big book of halloween fun

susie johns

BARRON'S

cOntents

16   Chapter 1: Costumes & Disguises

56   Chapter 2: Pumpkin Craft

80   Chapter 3: Creative Halloween Crafts

Introduction

The history of Halloween

The Celts in Britain had festivals for two major gods—a god of the sun and a god of the dead, who was called Samhain. A special festival named after Samhain was held each year on November 1st, the beginning of the Celtic New Year. The festival, which lasted for three days, marked the end of the season of the sun and the beginning of the season of darkness and cold.

On October 31st, the eve of Samhain, after the crops had all been harvested and stored for the long winter, the cooking fires in people's homes were extinguished. The Druids —Celtic priests—met on hilltops, among dark, sacred oak trees, where they lit bonfires and offered sacrifices of crops and animals. The word "bonfire"—originally "boon-fire"—means a huge fire built to honor the spirits of the air, to invoke favors, and to drive off evil spirits.

The next morning, the Druids handed out embers from their fires so people could start new cooking fires in their houses; these fires were meant not only to keep the homes warm, but also free from evil spirits.

The Romans, who invaded Britain in the first century, brought with them many of their own festivals and customs. One of these was the festival known as Pomona Day, named after their goddess of fruits and gardens, and celebrated around November 1st.

After hundreds of years of Roman rule, the customs of the Roman Pomona Day and the Celtic Samhain festival became integrated. The rituals of Pomona Day included apples, nuts, and a celebration of the harvest rituals, while some of the festivities during Samhain included magic, evil spirits, and death.

As Christianity took hold in Britain, the festival of Samhain was gradually incorporated into Christian ritual. In A.D. 835, the Roman Catholic Church declared November 1st to be a church holiday to honor all the saints. It was called All Saints' Day, also known as Hallowmas, or All Hallows' Day: in Old English, the word "hallow" meant "sanctify." Years later, the Church made November 2nd a holy day. It was called All Souls' Day and was a time to honor the dead. It was celebrated with big bonfires, parades, and dressing up. It introduced the elements of spirits and ghosts, skeletons and skulls to the Halloween melting pot.

Over time, October 31st became known as All Hallows' Eve, or Hallowe'en; Halloween is the modern spelling of the word. In Wales, Halloween is known as *Nos Galen-gaeof*, meaning the Night of the Winter Calends.

Halloween is not exclusively a Celtic tradition, however. Cultures all over the world have rituals and festivals at the end of October and the beginning of November. One of the most notable is the *Fiesta de los Muertos* in

Children should always be accompanied by an adult when trick-or-treating.

Children should be supervised at all times when making any projects or recipes in this book.

Mexico, where families have picnics in cemeteries, decorating relatives' graves with flowers and ribbons.

In India they celebrate Diwali, a Hindu holiday, on November 2nd. Just like the Irish custom of keeping candles in the window at Halloween, the traditional way to mark Diwali is to light candles and kerosene oil lamps.

Dressing up

Why do people dress up at Halloween? Well, the origins of this ritual go back a long way: dressing up is one of the customs that has been passed down through the centuries.

During the ancient festival of Samhain, the druids would parade in costumes made from the skins and heads of animals. Later, during the Christian festival of All Souls' Day, people would dress as saints, angels, and devils.

Trick or treat

The well-known custom of going from door to door demanding "treats" is one of the many rituals that has origins reaching far back in time.

Samhain marked the first day of winter; the eve of the festival was a time for settling bills. Workmen were given their wages and rents were expected to be paid.

In Ireland, it was a common practice to knock on doors collecting money, bread, cakes, nuts, and apples. Another Irish custom was to beg for "soul cakes" in exchange for blessings and promises of prosperity, or

protection against bad luck. This is probably where the "trick" element comes from. Even today, trick-or-treaters will threaten householders with mischief if they do not hand over sweets or money or some other trinket.

Since the Irish believed that fairies—or "little people"—were abroad on the night of Halloween, playing pranks and causing mischief, many people would leave an offering of food or milk on the steps of their house. This meant that the occupants would then be blessed with good luck for the coming year. So, by dressing up and going trick-or-treating today, you are taking the place of fairies and spirits who, it was believed, had the power to curse or bless any householders they visited on Halloween.

The Irish and the Scots called Halloween the "night of mischief." Boys would assemble in gangs and visit neighborhood houses, causing a great disturbance. Householders would be expected to bribe them with treats to make them go away.

Emigrants from Ireland and Scotland took these customs across the Atlantic—and, today, trick-or-treating is more prevalent in the United States than anywhere else in the world.

Food and drink

Eating and drinking are an important part of any festival—and Halloween is no different.

Because part of the tradition of Halloween centers around the harvest, it is no surprise that seasonal foods play a large part and, because of the colder weather at this time of year, this food is designed to be warming and welcoming. Winter vegetables are turned into soups and stews. Apples feature heavily in many dishes. Pumpkin recipes make use of the flesh that is scooped out when you carve your pumpkin to make a jack-o'-lantern.

November 2nd is All Souls' Day, the time to honor the souls of the dead. In Mexico, picnics and parties are an important part of the ritual so you could celebrate Halloween with Mexican food such as empanadas, burritos, enchiladas, chili con carne, and other delicious dishes.

If you turn to page 114 you will find a whole chapter full of recipes and ideas for festive Halloween food, some of it traditional and some merely inventive.

Witches and fairies

All over Europe—during medieval times and later—people believed that elves, fairies, and witches roamed around on All Hallows' Eve. The people would light bonfires to ward off these spirits.

Folklorists have chronicled how, at Halloween, hobgoblins, evil spirits, and fairies were busy abducting mortals and taking them off to fairyland, never to be seen again by their friends or family.

If they met fairies on All Hallows' Eve, British people believed they could throw the dust from under their feet at them, and they would be required to surrender any humans they were keeping captive. To avoid trouble

from fairy folk, people traveling distances on All Hallows' Eve would carry a black-handled knife or a steel needle for protection.

In Ulster, Northern Ireland, folklore chronicles how fairies were believed to be fallen angels. On All Hallow's Eve, oatmeal and salt were put on children's heads to protect them from evil and harm.

Witches have a long history with Halloween. Legends tell of witches gathering twice a year when the seasons changed, on April 30th—the eve of May Day—and on October 31st.

They would travel, the legends stated, on broomsticks, to celebrate a party hosted by the Devil. On the way, they cast spells on unsuspecting mortals, or they transformed themselves into different creatures.

These beliefs were not confined to Britain. In Europe, during medieval times and later, people believed that elves, fairies, and witches—who were supposed to occasionally take the shape of cats—took to the skies on All Hallows' Eve, and they would light bonfires to ward off these evil spirits.

Fire and flame

Candles and bonfires are an integral part of Halloween. In Irish homes it was the practice to light candles at Halloween—one for each deceased relative—in the room where the death occurred. It was also an Irish custom to keep candles in the window at Halloween.

In Britain, bonfires are associated more

with November 5th, in commemoration of English conspirator Guy Fawkes and a 1605 plot to blow up the Houses of Parliament in London. Being so close to Halloween, the divisions between the two are often blurred, with many people throwing parties around this time where they light bonfires, dress up, and enjoy a feast of hot soup, sausages, and baked potatoes.

Fortune-telling

Halloween was also traditionally a time for marriage divination. Country folk performed all kinds of rituals. For example, a young girl wishing to discover clues to her future marriage would peel an apple in one long, continuous strip, then drop the peel on the floor, hoping that it would form the initials of her future husband. Or she would stand in front of a mirror, eating an apple and hoping that his handsome face would appear, looking over her shoulder.

The tradition of bobbing for apples was also used as a way of forecasting whom a young person would marry.

Apples were not the only crops used in fortune-telling. A country girl would sweep around the base of a corn stack with a broom three times in the hope that, on the third time around, her future partner would appear or his name would be spoken aloud.

Even pulling cabbages was supposed to reveal information about a future spouse. Girls would be blindfolded and sent out in pairs to pull the first cabbage they found. If there was a lot of earth attached to the root, they would have plenty of money but if there was only a little dirt, they would be poor. They would then eat the cabbage and the flavor of its heart, sweet or bitter, would indicate the future husband's nature.

British people believed that the wind at midnight on All Hallows' Eve was believed to indicate the prevailing wind for the coming season. If there was a moon on Halloween, it was believed to be an omen. A clear moon meant fine weather. Clouds racing across the face of the moon meant that storms were on the way.

Halloween today

These days, Halloween is not all about being scared, celebrating the harvest, or predicting the future. Most people associate it with dressing up, playing games, having a party, enjoying festive food and drink, and going around the neighborhood, trick-or-treating. And most of us associate Halloween with carving a pumpkin into a jack-o'-lantern, to place in the window or on the front porch.

Planning a Party

It's fun to go to a party at Halloween—and even more fun to throw one of your own! But you can have a great party without spending too much money. It just takes a little ingenuity.

If you are having the party at home, remember that all children make a mess when they are having fun. Pick up the rug and cover the table with a plastic tablecloth, and warn the guests' parents in advance so their little ones don't get dressed up in their Sunday best.

When it's time to eat, don't use the best china—disposable plates, cups, and napkins are best because, after they have eaten their fill, the entire contents of the party table can be swept into plastic trash bags.

If space is at a premium, an indoor picnic can work very well. Put an old sheet or tablecloth on the floor for the children to sit around. Outside, if the weather allows, small children can be given a picnic lunch: put a wrapped sandwich, a cake, chips, fruit, and a drink in a little box or paper bag for each child.

For small children, serve small food: cut sandwiches into small pieces, cheese into cubes, and so on.

Older children may prefer a buffet-style meal where they can help themselves to what they like. Make provisions for vegetarians, children with special dietary needs, or allergies—and just plain fussy eaters.

If you are planning some form of entertainment, feed the guests first. Don't serve food, ice cream, or other refreshments once the entertainment has begun, or the food is likely to end up on the floor.

When planning games, try to choose them to suit the age group of the guests. Older children may enjoy sophisticated games, but younger ones will probably prefer to bounce around to some lively music. Dim the lights, too, and put up decorations.

But remember, at Halloween, while some young guests will enjoy a spooky atmosphere, some will be frightened, so make sure one of the rooms is well lit and welcoming.

Six weeks before the party:

* Make a guest list. Plan for an adult to accompany each pre-school child.
* Make or buy invitations (see page 112).
* Choose a theme for the party.
* If you are not holding the party at home, book a venue—a church hall, the local swimming pool, a movie theater, or bowling alley, perhaps.
* Hire an entertainer—choose one who will fit in with your party theme, such as a wizard.

Five weeks before the party:

* Send out your invitations.
* Place your order at the bakery for a Halloween cake.

Four weeks before the party:

* Ask a friend, family member, or neighbor for help on the day of the party—perhaps a teenager who might like to earn a little pocket money.
* Plan your costume (see Chapter 1 for ideas).
* Put together a box of spare clothes, hats, scarves, and other accessories for anyone who doesn't come in costume.

Two weeks before the party:

* Buy disposable plates, cups, and flatware.
* Buy balloons and streamers.
* Make some decorations (see Chapter 3 for ideas).

One week before the party:

* Call anyone who has not replied to your invitation, to check if they are coming.
* Plan the music: record a tape, CD, or digital party soundtrack.

Two days before the party:

* Buy the food and drink.
* Start preparing any dishes that can be made in advance—such as cakes and pastries.
* Make sure you have a camera to record the event.

The day before the party:

* Clear the furniture from the party room (if you are having the party at home).
* Put away any treasured possessions that might get damaged. This includes expensive rugs, cushions, and ornaments. Put dust covers over the couch and armchairs.
* Allocate a table for food, one for drinks, and one for presents.
* For small children, set out a low table for eating; they can sit on cushions.
* Decorate the party room to give it a festive feel. Use balloons and paper streamers to add a splash of color for minimum cost.
* Do any other advance food preparation.

On the day of the party:

* Childproof the party area and any rooms the guests have access to, including the bathroom.
* Close the doors of rooms children are not allowed into; lock them if necessary.
* Put nervous pets in an upstairs bedroom with a bowl of water and shut the door.
* Put the finishing touches on the food. Just before guests arrive:
* Put on your costume.
* Put on some music.
* Dim the lights and let the fun begin!

Trick-Or-Treating Safety

If you are out and about trick-or-treating this Halloween, it's important to follow a few basic safety rules. Here are a few guidelines which children and parents should bear in mind when trick-or-treating is on the agenda. And remember, don't eat all your treats at once!

Children must always be accompanied by an adult.

* For youngsters under the age of twelve, attach their names, addresses, and telephone numbers (including the area code) to their clothes where it will be easily visible.

* Stick to your neighborhood, where you know the area and people recognize you.

* Walk on the sidewalk, not in the road, even on the quietest street.

* Walk from house to house—don't run, in case you fall.

* Be careful when crossing lawns and rough, uneven ground.

* Take care when crossing roads.

* Plan and discuss your intended route with parents or caregivers and make sure they know the names of your companions.

* Visit only those houses that are well lit.

* Never enter a stranger's home.

* Carry some change, a phone card, or cell phone, in case of an emergency.

* Wear warm clothes if the weather is cold. Try not to choose a skimpy costume but, if you do, take a coat or wear some warm underwear.

* If your costume is long, make sure you don't trip.

* If you are wearing a dark-colored costume, add a few strips of reflective tape for visibility.

* Carry a flashlight or glowstick to help you find your way on dark pathways. It will also allow you to be seen by other people.

* If you are wearing a mask, make sure it doesn't obscure your vision.

* Return home at an agreed-upon time.

* Knives, swords, or other accessories that are part of your costume should be made of cardboard or flexible plastic. Never carry sharp objects.

* Wait until you get home before eating any of the treats you have been given. An adult should check them first, to make sure they are safe to eat.

Chapter 1

Costumes & Disguises

Wonderful Wizardy Warlock

Wizards crop up all over the place in books and films—just think of *Harry Potter* or *Lord of the Rings*. This costume is quite simple and can be adapted to fit any size. Who says only girls can dress up as witches on Halloween and cast spells? Witches and wizards unite!

Tunic

Choose a suitable black tunic or T-shirt; the one in this picture was a woman's black velvet tunic. Sew a row of stitches at both sides, about 4 in. (10 cm) from each side seam, to make it narrower. For a decoration, cut a spiral of purple felt (see template on page 178) and stitch in place.

Wand

Push a wooden dowel into a styrofoam ball. Wind shiny metallic sticky tape around the dowel. Brush the ball with craft glue and dust with purple glitter, shaking off the excess and leaving it to dry.

Finishing touches

You may like to wear pants or leggings under the tunic, especially on a cold night.

Hat

See page 22 for instructions. Use felt in a color to match the lining of your cloak—in this case, purple.

Did you know?
The male version of a witch is sometimes called a wizard or a sorcerer—and sometimes a warlock, which is a derivation of the Saxon word "war-loek," meaning oath-breaker.

Cloak

Cut a semicircle of black fabric and one of satin lining, each with a diameter of 30 in. (75 cm)—or larger, for a longer cloak. If the fabric is not wide enough, you'll have to join two or more pieces together before cutting. Stitch the two fabrics together, with right sides facing, along the straight edge, then turn right side out. In the center of the straight edge, stitch a band of fabric measuring $17\frac{5}{8} \times 3\frac{5}{8}$ in. (44 x 9 cm) and fold it over to form a neckband, stitching a hook and eye or snap fastener in place to fasten it around your neck. Hem the curved edge of both cloak and lining separately.

Wicked Witch of the West

Witches were believed to gather at Halloween to celebrate a party hosted by the Devil. The costume of a witch is classic Halloween wear and there are so many variations on the theme. The witch below is quite traditional, with a striking red twist in the gloves and boots. For a glamorous witch, see page 24.

Hat

The reason that a witch's hat is cone-shaped is to direct energy from higher dimensions to her mind and down through her body. You can make your own pointed hat from posterboard or fabric—you'll find full instructions on page 22.

Cloak

Take a rectangle of fabric—craft stores sell a variety of Halloween prints—measuring about 44 x 26 in. (1 m x 65 cm). (You can make it larger if you like.) Fold over one of the long edges and stitch. Thread a length of ribbon through the tube you have just created and pull it up to gather. Tie the ends of the ribbon around your neck.

Did you know?

The broom symbolizes the link between home life and travel to other spiritual dimensions—which is why witches were said to travel through the air on broomsticks.

Dress

You may have a suitable plain black dress, or a skirt and top. The witch in the picture is wearing a black jersey skirt that has been cut into strips all along the hem for a ragged effect, with a black and silver cardigan.

Finishing touches

Red panty hose and red fingerless gloves are eye-catching accessories, along with some pointy-toed boots and perhaps some unflattering glasses. Backcomb your hair (hold your hair from the ends, and comb it upwards) so it looks as though you have been dragged through a hedge. Buy a rubber snake and wrap it around your arm, and carry a broomstick and a cauldron (for instructions on how to make a Papier Mâché Cauldron, see page 100).

Horrible Heads & Hands

Simple accessories are often the key to a successful costume: if all you have to wear is a black dress or black pants and a T-shirt, add a pointed hat and you will be immediately transformed into a witch or a wizard.

Magic hat

Cut out a large circle of black felt, 15½ in. (39 cm) in diameter, then cut a hole out of the center, 6 in. (15 cm) in diameter. This will form the brim of the hat. Cut a quarter-circle of felt with a radius of 14½ in. (36 cm), curl it into a cone, and stitch the two straight sides together. Stitch the cone to the brim. This hat should fit a child up to the age of 10. For a larger hat, cut a circle 17¼ in. (43 cm) in diameter, with an inner hole of 6¾ in. (17 cm) in diameter. The cone should have a radius of 19¼ in. (48 cm).

   If you are not sure of your measurements, first cut these shapes from newspaper, tape the pieces together, and try on the hat. Make any necessary adjustments before cutting the pieces from felt—that way, you can be sure of a good fit without wasting valuable fabric.

Quick and easy hat

Follow the measurements given opposite but cut your hat pieces from construction paper or posterboard and glue or tape them together.

Talons

Fake nails can be very effective and make your hands look suitably sinister. They are available to buy from most drugstores, grocery and department stores, and party stores. If you have long nails anyway, you could just paint your own. To steady your hand, rest your wrist on the edge of a table to keep it steady, then, starting with your little finger, paint a stripe of polish in a single stroke up the center of your nail from base to tip. Quickly follow this with two more stripes, one on either side. Repeat with your other nails, then do the other hand. Let them dry before doing anything, or they might smudge.

You can also buy fake fingers in party stores. Made from plastic, they slip over your own fingers for an almost instant transformation.

Glamorous Witch

To dress up as a witch, you don't have to be a hag. Why not go for glamour instead? According to legend, if you want to meet a witch on Halloween night, you should put on your clothes inside out and walk backwards.

Dress

A plain black party dress is ideal.

Cloak

Instead of the usual style of cloak (see the Wonderful Wizardy Warlock on page 18 and the Wicked Witch of the West on page 20), take a few yards of stretchy black lace, wind it around your body, then drape it over one arm. If the weather turns cold, you can always wrap it around your head and shoulders.

Wand

As for the Wonderful Wizardy Warlock on page 18, make a wand from a wooden dowel wound around with sparkly sticky tape and topped with a styrofoam ball, this time studded with sequins.

Hat

The instructions for a basic hat, made from felt, are to be found on page 22. For added glamour and sparkle, wind some glittery gold net fabric around it.

Finishing touches

Long black evening gloves, black lace or fishnet panty hose, and high-heeled black shoes, plus a little makeup and some colored spray in your hair, will complete the outfit.

Witch legends

Witches have long been associated with Halloween. Legends tell of witches gathering twice a year when the seasons changed, on April 30th—the eve of May Day, and on the eve of October 31st—All Hallows' Eve. The witches arrived on broomsticks to celebrate at a party hosted by the Devil. Superstitions told of witches casting spells on unsuspecting people, transforming themselves into different forms, and causing other magical mischief.

Early witchcraft

There are many stories and myths about witches—people have always been fascinated by them. In its early days, witchcraft centered around nature—especially the sun, moon, and stars. Witches were thought to commune with trees, birds, animals, and seasonal cycles. Native American witch doctors were specialists in spiritual healing. When a person became ill, it was believed that some evil had entered his or her body—and the witch doctor sought to cure the person by casting out this evil. When Europeans came and settled in America, their practices and those of the Native American "witches" were combined.

In Europe between the 1400s and the 1700s, witches were maligned as evil Satan-worshippers who defied Christianity and engaged in dangerous and occult practices.

Witches were often persecuted. To "prove" whether or not a woman was a witch, she was ducked under water. If she floated, she was thought to be a witch. If she drowned, she was innocent—either way, the unfortunate woman died. Many innocent people were cruelly treated because of people's fear of witchcraft.

The Salem witch trials

In 1691, a spate of witchcraft trials wreaked havoc and hysteria in Salem Village, Massachusetts. When two young girls, Betty Parris and Abigail Williams, started to engage in macabre fortune-telling and displayed strange, hysterical behavior, they were branded as witches. When asked to identify who bewitched them, the girls named their neighbors, and soon, dozens of villagers were being accused of witchcraft and taken to court. Those who supposedly practiced witchcraft had been seen to mumble words (like spells), or to scream and fall to the floor as if suffering a fit; one "witch" claimed she saw red rats, talking cats, and a tall man dressed in black. By the end of 1692, nineteen people had been sentenced to death as a result of these trials.

"Witches" today

These days, the term "witch" can be used to describe a follower of the Wiccan religion—but these people are friendly witches! Although

Wiccans claim to use magic of sorts, they are not allowed to use it to harm anyone.

On April 30th, Germans celebrate Walpurgis Night, when witches are said to ride to meet their master, the Devil. The night of October 31st is, of course, Halloween, or All Hallows' Eve, the day before All Hallows' Day or All Saints' Day. It is the traditional time for witches to be at the height of their powers.

Hocus Pocus

Everyone knows that witches are supposed to be able to cast spells and transform people into different forms. Would you like being turned into a frog? What would you turn your friends into if you had the power?

Three of the most famous witches appear in *Macbeth*, a play by Shakespeare. These ugly, withered creatures with wild-looking hair and flowing dark cloaks were able to foretell the future. As they cast spells, they added nasty ingredients to a magical potion and chanted the following words:

> Double, double toil and trouble;
> Fire burn and cauldron bubble.
> Eye of newt, toe of frog,
> Wool of bat and tongue of dog,
> Adder's fork and blind worm's sting,
> Lizard's leg and howlet's wing.

Not all witches in fairy stories are wicked. There are tales about some witches who try to use their powers to help people rather than harm them. Instead of poisonous potions, they make medicines out of healing herbs.

Witches were reported to take to the skies and head to their midnight gatherings astride not only broomsticks, but goats, oxen, sheep, dogs, and wolves, as well as shovels and staffs.

It was thought that witches could be prevented from flying off, or could be brought down, by the peal of church bells. In the early seventeenth century, one German town was so fearful of witches that, for a time, churches rang their bells continuously from dusk until dawn in an effort to keep witches at bay.

The black cat has long been associated with witches. Many superstitions have evolved about cats. It was believed that witches could change into cats. Some people also believed that cats were the spirits of the dead. If a black cat crossed your path you had to turn around and go back, because if you continued, it was thought that bad luck would strike you.

Did you know?

The last person to be executed in Europe for being a witch was Anna Goddi. She was hanged in Switzerland in 1782.

Cute & Colorful Kitty

The perfect companion for any witch is a cat. Break with tradition and, instead of dressing as a black cat, conjure up a more colorful creation. Choose any color you like for a unique costume that'll make you stand out from the crowd! Just remember to wear a warm coat when you go trick-or-treating.

Costume

Wear a leotard and panty hose in any color. Make paws by stitching simple mittens from fleece fabric and edge them with swansdown. Tie short lengths of swansdown around your ankles, too. To make ears, copy the template on page 178 and cut out the shapes from fleece and felt, then stitch them to a headband. Add yet more swansdown trim, then tie some more around your hips to transform yourself into a really fluffy feline.

Did you know?

Witches don't work solo: they have "familiars," animal companions who carry out their wishes. The most common of these is the black cat. If a black cat crosses your path this Halloween, beware, as it might cast a spell on you. In North America, it is believed to be bad luck if a black cat crosses your path but in Britain and Ireland, it means good luck!

Makeup

You will need

Face paints in shades of lilac, violet, blue, white, and black   Makeup sponge paintbrushes, broad and fine
Hairband

1 Tie your hair back, away from your face. Sponge your whole face, except the area around your mouth and eyes, with lilac face paint.

2 With a broad, flat brush, paint in cat's eyes and a muzzle with white face paint.

3 Now use violet to draw a thick line on your eyelids and the lower edge of your cat's eyes; use blue to outline your muzzle and to give expression to your eyebrows.

4 Use violet to paint in stripes all around the edge of your face and black to paint in a nose and whiskers.

SAFETY NOTE:
Before you go to bed, make sure you clean off all your makeup or you'll end up with bleary eyes and smudges all over your pillowcase! Use soap and water or baby wipes to remove water-based face paints.

Beastly Cave Dweller

This primitive outfit is quickly and easily created from a length of animal print fabric. You could watch *The Flintstones* for inspiration. The club makes a great accessory that'll help you get into the spirit of being an authentic cave dweller.

Costume

You will need about 2 yards (2 m) of animal print fabric—choose something with a plush pile. Cut off a few strips to use for wristbands and headbands, and a long, wide strip for a belt, then wrap the rest of the fabric around you, tying it in place with the belt.

   Mess up your hair, smudge brown makeup on your cheeks, and carry a big club. To create wild hair, try backcombing it, strand by strand. Hair gel is useful, too, for helping to spike up your hair.

SAFETY NOTE: Children must be supervised when using scissors and glue.

Club

Make a great caveman's club from papier mâché.

You will need

Empty plastic bottle	Sticky tape
Cardboard tube (from paper towel)	White glue
Newspapers	Thick paintbrush
Scissors	Brown acrylic paint

1 Slit the cardboard tube and slip it over the neck of the plastic bottle; tape it firmly in place.

2 Roll up sheets of newspaper and wrap them around the bottle, taping them in place, to create a lumpy shape.

3 Dilute the glue with an equal amount of water and brush it over the club. Cover with torn strips of newspaper. Repeat until you have built up about four layers, then leave to dry.

4 When the papier mâché is dry, paint the club brown all over.

Bride of Frankenstein

Dress

For this creepy character, use an old wedding dress or white nightdress. See if you can find something suitable in a thrift store or rummage sale, which you can rip to make it torn and tattered.

Veil

Use a piece of white netting or lace. An old white net curtain is ideal because you can tear the edges. Tie your hair in a ponytail on top of your head, gather up one edge of the netting and pin it to your hair, then add white feathers, a flower, or both.

Finishing touches

Wear long gloves if you like, or perhaps you would prefer to stick on fake nails and paint them blood-red. White fishnet or lace panty hose will also add to the bridal theme.

Makeup

Sponge white face paint all over your face, including your mouth, eyebrows, and eyelids. Paint in new eyebrows using black face paint and a brush, or a black eyebrow pencil. Paint eyelids and the area under your eyes with brown to create a sunken, haunted look. Use a brush and red lipstick or face paint to create a thin-lipped, unsmiling mouth.

Frankenstein was a character invented in 1818 by the English writer, Mary Shelley, for a ghost story competition. In the early 1800s, scientists would sometimes steal bodies from graves in order to dissect and study them.

Mary Shelley hoped her story would warn of the dangers of such experiments. In the novel, Dr. Victor Frankenstein, fascinated by the workings of the human body, works day and night to create a person using dead body parts taken from graveyards, and then brings it to life using electricity from a bolt of lightning. The person he creates looks like a monster.

Frankenstein's monster is frightening to look at and, due to people's rejection and cruel treatment, becomes a murderer. One of the messages of the story is not to treat others badly just because of their appearance.

Many films have been made about Frankenstein and his monster. One of the most famous, released in 1931, starred actor Boris Karloff as the monster and was one of the first horror movies ever made.

The Bride of Frankenstein was Elizabeth, who married Victor only to be murdered in her bed the very next night, strangled by the monster that her husband had created.

Pumpkin Print T-Shirt

Your idea of dressing up may not involve changing your character. If you don't want to wear a "silly" costume, you could always decorate your regular clothes. In this case, a printed T-shirt may be just what you need. Worn with jeans, you can be comfortable and, at the same time, feel festive.

Turn to page 74 for instructions on how to make a pumpkin stamp. Follow the method for printing wrapping paper but instead of using acrylic paint, use fabric paint on a plain cotton T-shirt. Wash the T-shirt first, if it is new, to help the paint adhere to the fabric. Before printing, place a few sheets of newspaper inside the T-shirt so that when you print the front of the shirt, the paint does not soak through to the back.

SAFETY NOTE:
Children must be supervised when using a hot iron.

Other ideas

Cut Halloween motifs from fabric and pin them to your sweatshirt or the back of your jacket. For a more permanent decoration, stick fabric cutouts in place with fabric glue, or use an iron-on bonding material.

You could also dye items of clothing. If you haven't got enough black clothes, for example, try dyeing old cotton pants, socks, or a tracksuit with black dye.

When buying fabric paints, ask for advice. You will need water-based paints that are permanent and suitable for cotton fabrics. You will probably need to press your printed garment with a hot iron when the fabric paint has dried, to ensure that the color doesn't bleed or wash out when you put it in the washing machine.

Mucky Medieval Peasant

Take yourself back to the time when people believed in witchcraft by dressing as a poor peasant. Finish off the outfit by carrying a fake rat, and smearing makeup on your face to make it look dirty.

Tunic and pants

Search your local thrift store—or the cabinets at home—for a suitable sweater to transform into a tunic; bouclé yarns look a little like sheepskin. The tunic worn in this picture is a woman's bouclé cardigan, which had a tie belt and pockets that were removed and made into a little pouch. The front of the cardigan was sewn together from the hem to halfway up, and the opening laced with a leather thong. The leggings are cotton jersey pajama, bound at the ankles with strips of matching fabric.

Hood

Cut two rectangles of linen cloth, each measuring 32 x 16 in. (80 x 40 cm). On each piece, stitch together the two short ends to make a tube. Put one of the tubes over your head and let it drape over your shoulders. The other can be draped over your head to form a cowl.

Finishing touches

A rough strip of leather, cut from the ragged edge of a hide, makes a primitive belt. Carry a rubber rat—a plague rat—and go barefoot. Dirty your face by rubbing a finger in some brown eyeshadow and smudging it onto cheeks, forehead, and nose. For a really impoverished appearance, rub some under and around your eyes, too.

Eezy Zombies

You can give almost any of your old clothes the zombie treatment. Practice a slow swagger and a dazed look and you're set to frighten the living daylights out of anyone you come across!

If you don't want to spend a lot of money on a costume but you have an old T-shirt or shirt you were about to throw out, it's easy to dress up as a zombie.

Use scissors to slash a series of rips in the garment. If there are pockets, unpick the seams and leave them half hanging off.

To make bloodstains, use whatever you have handy in the way of red paint, ink, or dye. You will probably be throwing the costume away after Halloween, so you don't have to use proper fabric dyes. Just brush your ink or paint onto the rips and slashes you have made.

Makeup

Sponge pale gray or green face paint all over your face and neck. Use darker gray to create sunken shadows around your eyes and lines down from the corners of your mouth.

Use red face paint and a brush to draw lines of scratches down your face and neck, to echo the slashes in your clothes.

For a black eye, dab red face paint over your eyelid and eye socket, and under your eye, as well as a little on your cheekbone, using a cotton swab. Go over your eyelids, top and bottom, with blue-gray face paint.

Truly Terrifying Mummy

A clever costume created from strips of muslin will make you look like you have just staggered from a pharaoh's tomb.

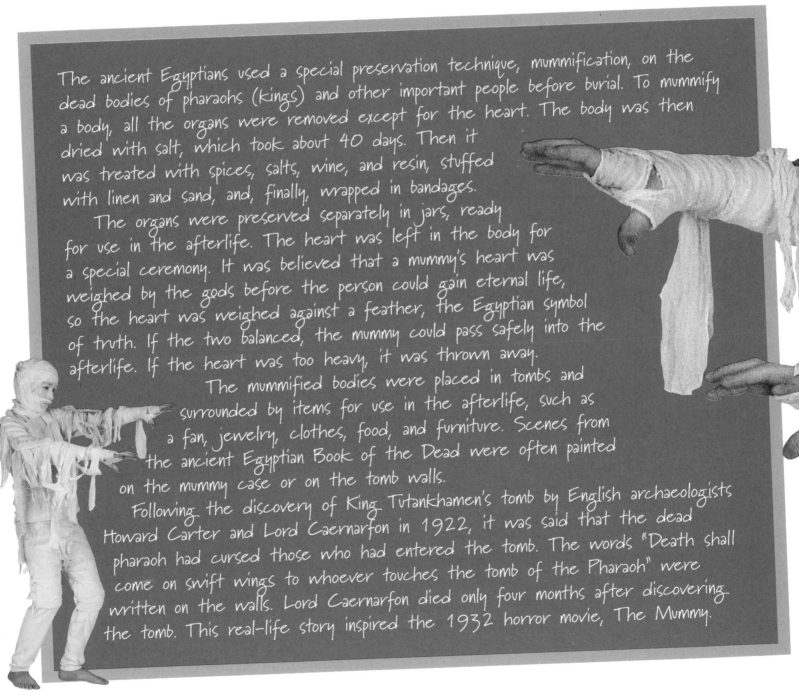

The ancient Egyptians used a special preservation technique, mummification, on the dead bodies of pharaohs (kings) and other important people before burial. To mummify a body, all the organs were removed except for the heart. The body was then dried with salt, which took about 40 days. Then it was treated with spices, salts, wine, and resin, stuffed with linen and sand, and, finally, wrapped in bandages.

The organs were preserved separately in jars, ready for use in the afterlife. The heart was left in the body for a special ceremony. It was believed that a mummy's heart was weighed by the gods before the person could gain eternal life, so the heart was weighed against a feather, the Egyptian symbol of truth. If the two balanced, the mummy could pass safely into the afterlife. If the heart was too heavy, it was thrown away.

The mummified bodies were placed in tombs and surrounded by items for use in the afterlife, such as a fan, jewelry, clothes, food, and furniture. Scenes from the ancient Egyptian Book of the Dead were often painted on the mummy case or on the tomb walls.

Following the discovery of King Tutankhamen's tomb by English archaeologists Howard Carter and Lord Caernarfon in 1922, it was said that the dead pharaoh had cursed those who had entered the tomb. The words "Death shall come on swift wings to whoever touches the tomb of the Pharaoh" were written on the walls. Lord Caernarfon died only four months after discovering the tomb. This real-life story inspired the 1932 horror movie, The Mummy.

Makeup

Sponge your face with white face paint. Use the strips of dyed muslin to wrap your head, hands, and feet.

Costume

It might be tempting to wrap your entire body in bandages, but think about the practicalities of getting undressed for bed after the party—not to mention visiting the bathroom.

The basis for this costume is a light-colored, long-sleeved jersey T-shirt and leggings—a set of long winter underwear would be ideal—plus about 6 yards (6 m) of muslin. The costume is easy to slip into and out of and can be used again and again.

Cut or tear the muslin into strips about 2½ in. (6 cm) wide. Stitch some of these strips overlapping each other on the body, sleeves, and legs of your jersey garments. Leave some of the ends dangling and don't worry about being too neat with your sewing.

Following the instructions on the dye packaging (remembering to wear gloves), make up a weak solution of brown dye and dip the costume, along with any spare strips of cloth, into the dye bath. Try to ensure that the dyeing process is uneven; don't leave the fabric in the dye for too long (you are aiming for a pale, aged effect, not dark brown).

Once you're happy with the result, wash the garments and strips of cloth in a washing machine and let them dry. The washing and drying process will help to fray and pucker the cotton.

Dressing Up Decisions

Dressing up is such an important part of Halloween for most people that they would not be seen dead in their everyday clothes! There are plenty of costumes you can throw together if you don't have much time—simply search through your wardrobe for old clothes and you're bound to get some ideas.

If you are going out trick-or-treating, or you have been invited to a Halloween party, you will have to dress up—no question.

If you are a bit of an exhibitionist, you probably cannot wait for Halloween to come around each year; if you are a little shy, however, you may be reluctant to put on an outfit that will to draw attention to yourself.

No matter how extravagantly you wish to dress, though, you may be held back by your budget—but a fabulous costume doesn't have to cost a lot. No matter what your outlook or your budget, there's a costume for you. These days, any kind of costume seems to be acceptable, as long as it is fancy dress. But you might prefer to stay true to the spirit of Halloween by dressing as a character connected with the ancient legends—a witch, druid, or peasant—or at least someone who is very scary, or very dead.

Other ideas

* **Pirate:** White shirt, knee breeches, boots, a jacket with brass buttons, a silk sash or a wide leather buckled belt, a headscarf with a three-cornered hat on top, a cutlass, and an ancient treasure map.

* **Druid:** A brown dressing gown, several sizes too big, with a hood, a belt, and sandals.

* **Outlaw:** Shirt, jeans, chaps if you have them, cowboy boots, black hat, a mask, a droopy mustache, and a scar.

* **Scarecrow:** Checkered shirt, patched jeans or dungarees, and an old tweed jacket held in place with lengths of rope tied around cuffs and waist. Add tufts of straw, paint your face white or yellow, and wear a straw hat.

* **Dracula:** An evening jacket worn with a cape, white face paint, and plastic fangs.

* **Skeleton:** Decorate a black leotard and panty hose with "bones" made from white tape or ribbon, glued or stitched in place.

* **Ghost:** An old white sheet with holes cut out for eyes.

* **Monster:** An oversized running suit stuffed with crumpled newspapers to create a misshapen silhouette. Add fake rubber feet and a hideous mask.

* **Devil:** Red leotard and panty hose with a tail and horns from a party store.

* **Nutty professor:** A lab coat over your normal clothes and a pair of wire-rimmed glasses.

Sources

Here are some ideas for places to find your Halloween costume...

* Thrift stores

* Flea markets

* For a few dollars, someone else's throwaway could be your must-have garment. Check around for out-of-date evening dresses, suits that have gone out of style, and bedspreads and curtains that can be cut up and sewn into creative costumes.

* Rummage sales

* Your wardrobe

* Sewing and tailor/seamstress shops

* At the end of the season, there are bargains to be found in most stores. In this chapter, a lot of the accessories—such as evening gloves, colored panty hose, and belts—were found in top-level stores at closeout prices.

* Boutiques that sell trendy clothes to appeal to teenagers often have fishnet and other novelty panty hose, unusual jewelry, colored hairsprays and nail polishes, as well as some rather extreme styles of clothing. It's worth a look.

* Closeout or going-out-of-business sales

* You may not think your everyday clothes have the potential to scare people—but a plain jogging suit or a simple dress can form the basis of a great outfit. Check out the wardrobes of other family members, too, for evening dresses, dinner suits, and smart accessories that can be put to use.

* Stores that sell fabrics are a great source of inspiration for Halloween costumes. In the months and weeks leading up to Halloween you will find novelty fabrics with spiders' webs, witches, and other Halloween motifs, but you will also find lace, satins, silks, felt, fleece, and all kinds of exciting materials just waiting for you to get your creative hands on them.

* Party stores—these are an essential provider of false noses, face paints, fairy wings, and accessories such as rubber rats, snakes, and spiders.

Green Grinning Goblin

A goblin, or hobgoblin, is a small, ugly creature who goes around playing tricks and making mischief. Goblins wear green so all you need to do is find yourself a few basic green garments and you're halfway to a successful costume. This cute outfit looks great on young children.

The costume in this picture started with a green sweater and a pair of short pants—but you might have some other basics handy, such as a leotard and panty hose or a jogging suit. To transform yourself into a goblin—or a gnome, elf, or pixie, for that matter—you just need to add a pointy hat and collar.

You don't have to be good at sewing to make a pointed hat. Just cut a quarter-circle of green felt with a radius of about 16 in. (40 cm) and stitch the two straight sides together. This should fit most children up to the age of twelve.

For a collar, cut a circle of green felt with a diameter of 15¼ in. (38 cm) and cut a circle from the center with a diameter of 5½ in. (14 cm). Using the template on page 178 as a guide, cut the outer edge into points. Cut a slit from the edge to the center so that you can get the collar around your neck; slip it onto your shoulders and pin it in place with a safety pin.

At Halloween, people were frightened that hobgoblins and other evil fairy folk would abduct their children and take them off to fairyland.

As well as goblins and hobgoblins, other mischievous creatures include gnomes who live underground, wear pointed hats, and guard treasure. Elves and pixies are small fairy folk with pointed ears who possess magical powers. Leprechauns are tiny men with magical powers who guard the pot of gold which is to be found at the end of the rainbow.

Finishing touches

Elves, pixies, gnomes, and goblins—even leprechauns—can all make use of green face paint, sponged over the face, neck, and ears. Use black face paint and a brush to create arched eyebrows which will give you an impish expression.

If you don't like the idea of painting your face, you can always spray your hair green. Look in your local drugstore for a colored hairspray can be brushed out later or removed by shampooing.

SAFETY NOTE:
Children should be supervised by an adult when using hairspray.

Bad Fairy

With clumpy boots instead of dainty shoes and a purple tutu instead of a white or pink one, you can be a fairy with attitude. Mix and match your accessories to create a unique outfit that'll dazzle everyone.

In Ulster, Northern Ireland, people believed that fairies were fallen angels. On Halloween night, oatmeal and salt were put on children's heads to protect them from harm.

Hey ho for Halloween
When the fairies all are seen,
Some black and some green.
Hey ho for Halloween!

(Traditional rhyme)

Dress

To make a tutu, you will need about 4 yards (4 m) of net and enough wide ribbon to go around you, just below your waist, with about one inch (2.5 cm) overlap. This skirt is quite easy to make, but you may require some adult help to gather the fabric.

Cut the net lengthwise into three strips. Take one strip and gather it along one edge so that it becomes the same length as the ribbon. Secure the gathered edge by passing a needle and thread through the netting. Do the same with the other two strips of net, then stitch all three to the ribbon, one above the other. Add hooks and eyes to the ends of the ribbon to fasten.

Wand

For a fairy wand, cut two star shapes from thick cardboard and glue them back to back with the end of a stick in between. Paint the star on both sides, brush with glue and dip in glitter, and wrap the stick with glittery sticky tape.

Finishing touches

Mess up your hair and go crazy with your makeup—black eyeliner and black or purple lipstick, for example. And don't forget a pair of wings from the local party shop!

Braveheart for Dads

Don't let the children have all the fun this year: dress up and have some Halloween fun of your own. Watch Mel Gibson in the film *Braveheart* for inspiration. For this costume, you need a length of tartan fabric, half a face of blue paint, and a lot of courage.

The shirt

Start with an old, loose-fitting checkered shirt. Remove the pockets and the collar. Cut off the button bands and sew up the front from the hem to about two-thirds of the way up. Stitch a gilt button on either side of the neck opening, put the shirt on, and wind a leather thong around the two buttons to fasten.

The kilt

Start with a piece of tartan 60 in. (1.5 m) wide and 3 yards (3 m) long. Cut it lengthwise into two pieces, the larger being a yard (1 m) wide. Wrap this wider piece around your waist, pleating it as you go, and hold it in place with a belt. Let the fabric fall over the top to hide the belt. Take the narrower piece and fling it over one shoulder, tucking the ends in the belt.

Be Halloween-friendly

* Welcome trick-or-treaters by putting up a friendly sign on your front door.
* Decorate the outside of your house with jack-o'-lanterns, banners, and wreaths.
* Have plenty of treats ready for the trick-or-treaters when they call.
* Let the neighbors' children know that they can make your house the last stop on their rounds, then make them welcome with a hot drink and something to eat.

Finishing touches

In *Braveheart*, Mel Gibson had long hair so you may want to wear a wig. You will also need to paint your face blue, using face paint and a small sponge or a wide, flat brush. Copy this picture or check out the film for yourself.

Mom's Glamorous Witch

Be the most glamorous witch at the party: black is so flattering! Why not throw a witches' and wizards' party, and ask all your party guests to dress accordingly—it's a great theme for an adults' Halloween party!

Dress

This is easy: just put on your favorite black dress, preferably one with a bit of sparkle.

Hat

You will find instructions for making a witch's hat on page 22. For an adult's head, you need to increase the size of the brim to 22 in. (55 cm) in diameter, with a hole 6¾ in. (17 cm) in diameter; for the cone-shaped top you need to cut a quarter-circle with a radius of 19¼ in. (48 cm). This makes a very tall hat indeed. Instead of felt, you could make your hat in a patterned fabric, in which case, cut two brims and two quarter-circles of fabric and put interfacing between the two layers to add a little stiffness.

When you have your own gathering of witches, make up some of your favorite punch recipe and serve from a cauldron.

Wand

See page 18 for instructions.

Robe

Find a black cardigan or even a slinky bath robe. The one in the picture is made of velour and already has a frill on the front edges—but you could add your own.

Then cut pieces of black sheer fabric into long points and stitch to the underside of each sleeve.

Chapter 2

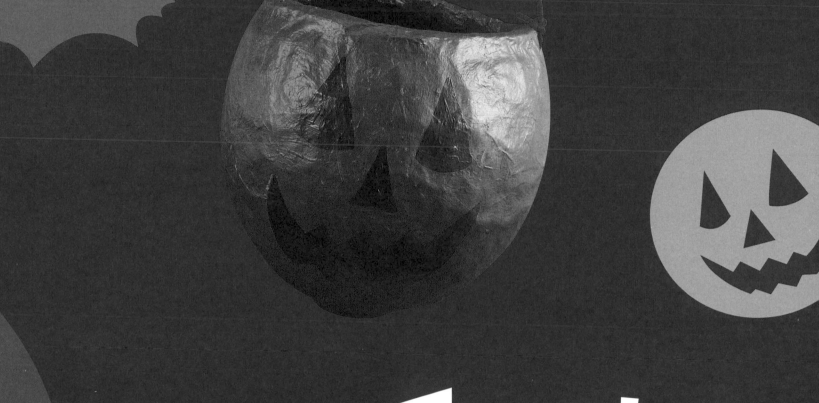

Pumpkin Craft

Basic Carving Techniques

The carving of pumpkin lanterns—jack-o'-lanterns—is an important part of the Halloween celebrations for almost everyone. The flickering candlelight cast by the lantern—the captive flame—illuminates the gloom and casts eerie shadows, while the leering carved face is quite scary!

Carving Tips

Pumpkins belong to the squash family, which includes hundreds of varieties of all shapes, sizes, and colors, including zucchini, marrows, and acorn, butternut, and turban squashes.

These vegetables are native to America. The tradition of eating pumpkin at Thanksgiving originated when the Pilgrim Fathers, who settled in New England, set aside a day of prayer and thanks for the harvest. They would serve a hollowed-out pumpkin which had been filled with milk, honey, and spices, and then baked.

The variety used to make Halloween lanterns is called the English pumpkin: orange-skinned, with soft flesh that is easy to scoop out. Select a pumpkin that is ripe and has no bruises, cuts, or nicks. Do not carry a pumpkin by its stem, as it may break.

**SAFETY NOTE:
Pumpkin carving can be a dangerous activity involving sharp tools and even small saws. Children must never be left alone while carving pumpkins and parents are strongly encouraged to do all cutting and carving themselves.**

TOOLS

Serrated knife or saw: Some pumpkins can be tough, so you might need a hacksaw to make the first cut through a hard pumpkin skin.

Spoon: For scooping out the seeds and flesh, a sturdy dessert spoon— or a melon scoop, if you have one—is ideal.

Apple corer: A tool designed to remove the core from a whole apple can be invaluable for gouging perfect round holes in the pumpkin shell.

Woodcutting tools: Printmaker's tools, usually used for gouging out patterns in wood or linoleum, are also ideal for carving patterns in pumpkins—especially for fine, delicate patterns.

Plastic pumpkin-carving knife: You may find special tools available at supermarkets during the pumpkin season. These are often safer for children to use.

You will also need a felt-tip marker to draw your design on the pumpkin before you start, a container to put the pulp and seeds into—you may like to roast the pumpkin seeds later— and some newspaper to avoid getting pumpkin pulp everywhere!

How to Carve a Pumpkin

1 If you don't want to get the table dirty, either place the pumpkin on layers of newspaper or do the carving outside. With a felt-tip marker, draw a circle on the top of the pumpkin, around the stalk. Draw a notch in the circle to make it easier to replace the lid when the carving is complete.

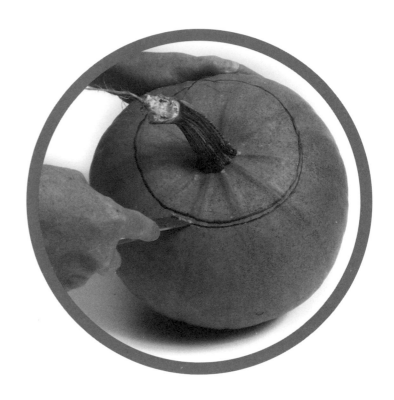

2 Cut along the outline of the circle using a sharp knife with a strong blade.

3 Pull the lid off the pumpkin and cut away the pulp and seeds.

4 Put your hand inside the pumpkin and pull out the seeds and stringy membranes.

5 Use a spoon or other suitable scooping tool to remove most of the flesh—which should be reserved for making pumpkin soup. You want the pumpkin shell to be about 1 in. (2.5 cm) thick to make carving easier.

6 Look carefully at your pumpkin to decide the best place to carve a face. Use a felt-tip marker to draw the features on the pumpkin. Then use a knife to cut out the features.

SAFETY NOTE: Adults must light any candles themselves and remember never to leave a lit candle unattended.

7 Finally, when your jack-o'-lantern is ready, place a tealight or candle inside and get an adult to light it. Then replace the lid and position your jack-o'-lantern in a prominent place in the house.

Pumpkin Faces

There are many variations on the jack-o'-lantern face. Some pumpkin carvers favor triangular eyes, while some prefer round ones; some like to give their pumpkin a cheeky grin while others insist on a snarl. The way you design your pumpkin face is often determined by the shape of the pumpkin and any lumps, bumps, and blemishes on its surface. Here are some variations on a theme: copy one of these or make up your own.

have a horrible HALLOWEEN!

Jack-O'-Lanterns

Jack was an Irishman—a drunkard—who made a pact with the Devil. The legend lives on in the pumpkin lantern that bears his name. Whether you carve one, cook one, or use one to inspire lots of different decorations, pumpkins are bound to feature in your Halloween celebrations.

The old Irish legend goes something like this...One day Jack was out in the woods, where he met the Devil. Jack managed to trick the Devil into climbing a tree to throw down some fruit for him. Once the Devil had thrown down the fruit, Jack carved a cross in the tree trunk, thereby trapping the Devil up in the branches. Jack then struck a deal with the Devil to leave his soul alone when he died. This backfired, though, because when Jack did die, Heaven would not take him in and, when he tried to get into Hell instead, the Devil would not let him through but handed him a burning ember. Jack carried the ember in a hollowed-out turnip, to light his way as he wandered through eternal darkness on Earth.

The jack-o'-lantern

For years, at Halloween, it was the custom to carry hollowed-out turnips carved to represent faces. This is the origin of the modern jack-o'-lantern.

Irish people who emigrated to America discovered how much easier pumpkins were to carve than turnips, so now the pumpkin lantern is the decoration we associate most with Halloween.

In recent years, pumpkin carving has turned into quite an art form as people carve not only fearsome faces into pumpkin shells, but all kinds of weird and wonderful designs.

In Somerset, England, the local people have their own tradition involving beet lanterns. On the last Thursday in October, the local people celebrate Punkie Night. It originated when a group of men from a town called Hinton St. George got drunk at a local fair and couldn't find their way home. The women went out to find their husbands, carrying lanterns made from hollowed-out mangel-wurzels, a kind of beet known locally as a "punkie." In subsequent years, children would parade through villages carrying punkie lanterns and singing a special song.

Easy Pumpkin Craft

The squash family, to which pumpkins belong, has many colorful and shapely varieties. One of these is the butternut squash. Its shell is the color of butter, and inside you will find juicy orange flesh that can be used in all kinds of recipes such as pumpkin soup (see page 130).

Here, three butternut squashes have been quickly transformed into Halloween heads. This method requires no cutting or carving, making it very quick and easy to do, even for the youngest members of the family. It also means that, once Halloween is over, the decoration can be washed off and the squashes cooked and eaten.

Use black poster paint and a medium-fine brush, or a poster paint pen, available from art suppliers, to paint a funny face on a butternut squash.

If you have more than one squash, you can paint a variety of different faces, making the expressions angry, scary, funny, or puzzled, then display them all in a row, indoors or out, on All Hallows' Eve.

Alternative Carving Ideas

If you have a particularly hard pumpkin, or you simply want to move away from the conventional jack-o'-lantern, why not try a different way of decorating a pumpkin. By decorating the surface of your pumpkin or other colorful winter vegetable, you can experiment with all sorts of designs.

For surface decoration, you will need some special tools. A do-it-yourself enthusiast may have fine chisels in the toolbox; a keen cook might have a tool called a canelle cutter; an artist might have linocutting or woodcutting tools: ask around, in case there is something suitable you can borrow. If not, treat yourself to a simple, inexpensive set of carving tools that will enable you to cut grooves of different widths and depths in the skin of a pumpkin.

Draw your design on the pumpkin before you start. The easiest way to do this is to trace a design onto paper, then use a pin to prick the design though the paper and onto the pumpkin's skin. This will give you a series of pinpricks to follow. You may prefer to draw your design freehand with a felt-tip marker; in this case, as you carve, you will follow the lines you have drawn, removing them as you go.

If you are new to the technique, stick to simple patterns and motifs: a bat, an owl, a snake, a cat, or a witch on a broomstick, for example. As well as pictures, you can carve out letters to spell out Halloween messages.

Experiment with different-colored pumpkins. Dark green ones are often the most effective, as the designs show up well as you reveal the pale flesh beneath the skin.

SAFETY NOTE:
When carving or decorating pumpkins using sharp tools, children should always be supervised by an adult.

Pumpkin Designs

While you have your carving tools at the ready, and a few spare squashes, why not try your hand at these stylish designs?

**SAFETY NOTE:
Only adults should
light candles.**

A pumpkin lantern doesn't have to have a face—in fact, it doesn't even have to be a pumpkin.

Start by hollowing out the pumpkin or other type of squash, as described on pages 60–61. Then use a small, sharp knife to cut out a star shape, or use a star-shaped metal cookie cutter, if you have one.

Use an apple corer to cut round holes right through the skin and flesh of your lantern. Use a linocutting tool, too, to gouge decorative stripes in the skin.

TIPS

✳ To keep a pumpkin lantern from drying out, cover it with a damp dish towel or washcloth when it is not on display.

✳ Tealights and candles create a flickering light when placed inside a lantern—but remember that naked lights are a fire hazard. Even outdoors, have sand or water handy to quench flames and never leave burning candles unattended.

✳ Pour some sand in the base of the lantern, then push a tealight or candle into the sand. This will help to prevent it from falling over and to extinguish the flame if the candle burns too low.

✳ The jack-o'-lantern itself should be put on a stable surface. If necessary, cut a slice off the bottom to make it stand firm.

Vegetable Faces

If the pumpkin you bought has gone moldy or if you are looking for other ways to display your creativity this Halloween, try making one of these veggie heads instead.

Halloween *is* a harvest festival—albeit a pagan one—so feel free to use other winter vegetables, not just pumpkins, to make lanterns or to assemble into hideous heads to grace the mantelpiece or porch at Halloween.

See what you have in your vegetable basket, then use your imagination to conjure up creative sculptural heads. The larger vegetables make the heads, with smaller specimens forming features, held in place with wooden toothpicks. It's fun to do and the heads can be dismantled after Halloween and the vegetables turned into a tasty winter stew.

Celery root has a gnarled appearance, making it a great base for a wizened head. In the picture, a baby corn cob makes a knobbly nose, a slice cut from a Scotch bonnet chili makes a mean mouth, and circles cut from a large zucchini give the eyes a sinister expression.

A rutabaga has a good surface for decoration, smooth but with the occasional fibrous wisp. Slice chilis and carrots for eyes, nose, mouth, and ears and top it off with a hat cut from the end of a large zucchini.

Turn a pumpkin on its side and use the base for a face. Baby corn cobs make great horns when inserted into holes created with an apple corer, and can be used for eyebrows, too. Use a carrot for a nose and, with chili pepper eyes and a mouth constructed of pieces cut from a large zucchini, the face is complete.

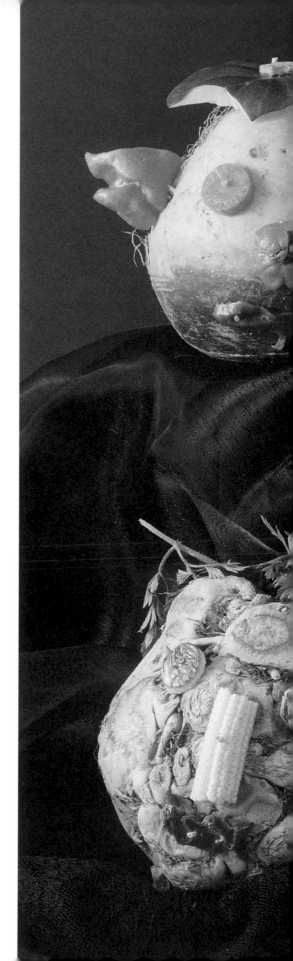

Papier Mâché Pumpkin

This pumpkin head is crafted from papier mâché. Use it as a decoration or carry it with you when you go trick-or-treating, to fill with goodies. Once you have mastered this project, it'll be easy to make the cauldron on page 100 and any other imaginative Halloween containers you can come up with.

You will need

A balloon	Lid from a jar
Small bowl	Adhesive tape
White glue	Acrylic paints in red,
Paintbrushes	yellow, and black
Newspapers	Ribbon or cord
Tissue paper	

This pumpkin head is made in the same way as the Papier Mâché Cauldron project on page 100—but without the legs. Consult the cauldron project for step-by-step pictures if you like. The lid from a jar—or even a circle cut from thick cardboard—is stuck on the bottom to create a flat base for the head to stand on.

1 Blow up a balloon to the size you want the finished head to be and tape it to a bowl for stability. Mix the glue with an equal volume of water and brush it over the balloon. Cover it with about eight layers of newspaper, torn into strips, adding diluted glue with each layer. Leave to dry. Then add about three more layers, this time using tissue paper, to create a smooth surface for painting.

2 When the paper is dry, burst the balloon and remove it. Trim the edge of the papier mâché shell, to give you the shape of a hollowed-out pumpkin.

3 Tape the lid to the base of the shell, so it will stand firm without toppling over. Cover it with a few layers of papier mâché.

4 Paint the head, inside and out, with orange paint made by mixing the red and yellow. Try to match the color with that of a real pumpkin, dabbing on different shades of orange and red for a realistic mottled effect. When this is dry, paint the features in black.

5 Make holes near the top, one at either side, and thread with a length of cord or ribbon, to make a handle.

If you are planning to use the head as a table centerpiece, you could place a battery-operated flashlight inside the head to create an eerie glow.

Pumpkin Potato Prints

You will need

Plain paper	Wooden block or small cardboard box
Craft foam	Black acrylic paint
White glue 	Roller

1 Trace the pumpkin motif from page 178 onto a scrap of paper and use this as a template for cutting out the shape from craft foam.

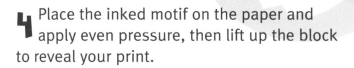

2 Stick the foam shape to a wooden block or a small, sturdy cardboard box. The printing block is now ready to use.

4 Place the inked motif on the paper and apply even pressure, then lift up the block to reveal your print.

3 Pour out a little paint onto a saucer and use a roller to apply it to the printing block.

5 Repeat as many times as desired.

TIPS

Use the paper to wrap Halloween gifts (see the picture on page 68), or print a large roll of orange paper and use it to decorate the walls of your party room on Halloween night.

You can use this method to decorate fabrics as well as paper. Print a Halloween T-shirt (see page 36) or print a length of cotton fabric to make into trick-or-treat sacks.

Pumpkin Ideas

The jack-o'-lantern is such an eye-catching design that you can use it as a motif to create all kinds of Halloween decorations.

Pumpkin balloons

Blow up orange balloons. Cut shapes from black paper—triangles for eyes and noses, and zigzags and crescents for leering mouths—and stick them on the balloons, using double-sided sticky tape, to create jack-o'-lantern faces. Use the designs on pages 62–63 for inspiration.

Pumpkin decals

You will find a number of pumpkin motifs on pages 62–63. Cut these from orange paper and stick them all over the house for a festive flavor.

Edible pumpkin decorations

Use pumpkin motifs to cut out pieces of rice paper (to decorate Halloween cakes) or rolled-out sugar paste (for cakes and cookies).

Pumpkin stencils

Transfer a pumpkin motif to a stencil card and stencil pumpkin patterns on windows, using a frosting spray, or on paper napkins and tablecloths, using paints.

Pumpkin stationery

Cut paper pumpkin motifs and use them to stick onto greeting cards, invitations, gift tags, and labels.

Paper Plate Mask

Making a mask from a paper plate is a simple, cheap, and effective idea. Use your creative skills to design other paper plate masks suitable for Halloween, such as a skull mask, using black and white paints, a red devil with cardboard horns stuck on, or a green goblin mask to go with the costume on page 48.

You will need

Paper plate	Paintbrush
Green posterboard	Scissors
Glue stick	Elastic
Acrylic paints in orange and black	

1 Paint the underside of the plate orange.

2 When the orange paint is dry, paint features in black. When dry, cut out around the sides and base of the nose shape, to create a flap. (Your nose will stick through the hole.)

3 Make a stalk and leaf shape out of green posterboard. Draw around the edge of the plate as a guide to size and shape, then draw a stalk and leaf shape and cut it out. Stick to the mask.

4 Make a hole in either side of the mask and thread with a length of elastic, long enough to fit snugly around your head.

Chapter 3

Creative Halloween Crafts

Creepy Door Wreath

For a wicked welcome on Halloween, decorate your door with a wreath of spooky spiders. Alternatively, add black and orange pipe cleaners contorted into alphabet letters to spell out a Halloween message—"Beware of ghosts" or "Witches welcome," for example.

You will need

Styrofoam ri	2 sheets of black craft foam
9½ in. (25 cm) in diameter	Self-adhesive labels (or white paper)
12 black pipe cleaners	White glue
15 white pipe cleaners	Googly eyes
1 pack orange crepe paper	Narrow ribbon, 26 in. (65 cm) long
Double-sided sticky tape	

1 Cut the crepe paper into 1½ in. (4 cm) strips and wind these around the ring, pulling the paper into folds as you go and fastening ends in place with double-sided sticky tape.

2 To make a spider's web, cut two white pipe cleaners in half. Lay the four pieces across each other and twist in the center to form a star with eight spokes. Join in a whole pipe cleaner by winding one end onto one of the spokes at about the halfway point, then twist it around each of the other spokes in turn, to make the inner ring. Do the same with another whole pipe cleaner, and another half, to create an outer ring. Make two more webs in the same way.

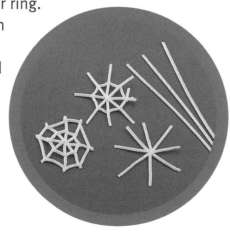

3 From the black craft foam, cut a circle 3¼ in. (8.5 cm) in diameter for each spider body and a leaf shape for each head. Cut teeth from white labels (or paper) and stick these in place on each body, then stick a head on top. Using double-sided tape, stick four black pipe cleaners to the back of each spider body and bend to form legs. Stick on googly eyes.

4 Tape the spiders and webs to the wreath. Tie the ends of the ribbon together and loop it around the ring, then hang up.

Other ideas

Try decorating a plain vine wreath (homemade, or an artificial one purchased from a garden center) by sticking on Halloween motifs cut from paper. Brush the wreath with glue and sprinkle it with glitter.

Candle Lamp

Switch off the lights and use candles to create an eerie Halloween glow. These custom-made candle lamps will cast some sinister shadows. Just remember always to let an adult light the candle for you and never leave burning candles unattended.

Candles are a part of Halloween tradition. For hundreds of years it was the custom in Ireland to light a candle at Halloween for each deceased relative in the room where the death occurred. Another Irish tradition was to put lighted candles on windowsills at Halloween. In India, the traditional way to mark Diwali, a festival which is celebrated at about the same time as Halloween, is to light candles and oil lamps.

You will need

Cylindrical glass vase	Hole punch (optional)
Black or dark-colored construction paper	Double-sided sticky tape
Scissors	Colored acetate (optional)
White posterboard	Sand
White (or light-colored) pencil	Candles

1 To make the bat candle lamp, cut a piece of black or dark-colored construction paper to fit around the outside of the vase with a ⅝ in. (1.5 cm) overlap. Trace the bat template from page 178 onto a small piece of posterboard, then cut this out and use it as a template.

To use the lamp, pour some sand in the base and place a tealight or candle in it.

To make the pumpkin candle lamp, first cut out the pumpkin shape (using the template on page 178), then add features separately, sticking these in place after the main piece of paper has been wrapped around the vase. You may like to wrap the vase in a sheet of colored acetate first.

2 Draw around the template three times, using the white pencil, then cut out the shapes. Use the scissors or a hole punch to cut out small circles—and stars, too, if you have a star-shaped punch. Wrap the paper around the vase and tape in place.

SAFETY NOTE:
Only adults should light candles and remember never to leave a lit candle unattended.

Doorknob Hanger

Make it clear whether or not you welcome visitors this Halloween by making a sign to hang on your doorknob. Be as friendly or as spooky as you like in your message...

You will need

Craft foam | Glue suitable for craft foam
Scissors

1 Trace the basic doorknob hanger shape from page 179. Transfer it to a sheet of craft foam and cut it out.

3 Cut out letters to spell out your Halloween message. (Ready-cut letters are available from good craft stores.)

2 To decorate the hanger, cut shapes from different colors of craft foam, using the templates you like from pages 178–179.

Other ideas

Make up your own message—how about, "At home to ghosts" if you want to encourage visitors, or "No entry to spooks" if you don't. Put a different message on each side of the hanger, in case you change your mind.

Instead of cutouts, why not add a scary photo of yourself making a nasty face, to frighten everyone away? On the other side, to accompany a welcoming greeting, you could glue on a smiling photo.

Warning bells

When you are getting ready for Halloween, you don't want unwelcome visitors bursting in on you. Thread bells onto a length of ribbon and tie the ends together to make a loop, then hang it on the inside of your door.

Window Silhouettes

Cut from black paper, these simple shapes create a spooky scene on a window. And they're dead easy to make too...

To make Halloween window decorations, cut out shapes such as bats, creepy castles, and pumpkins and attach them to the windows with a little double-sided sticky tape or non-permanent spray adhesive.

Simply trace or photocopy the shapes from pages 180–181 onto small pieces of posterboard and cut them out to make templates. You may wish to enlarge some of the shapes using a copy machine.

Draw around the templates on black construction paper or thin black posterboard, using a white or light-colored pencil. Use the lines you have drawn to cut out the shapes.

You could also stick small cutouts onto a lampshade (see page 96) to cast spooky shadows on the walls. The smaller shapes can be used to decorate greeting cards, place cards, and other items.

Did you know?

Spiders were believed to cure fever and whooping cough, and their webs were used to treat bleeding. Imagine having a fever, and being made to swallow a whole spider, perhaps covered in molasses or jelly, or having to wear a spider in a little linen bag around your neck! Spiders are also linked to various superstitions. Some people believe that if you kill a spider, it will rain the following day.

Table Mats

These personalized mats are an easy and inexpensive way of making your party guests feel welcome. Make place mats from paper and decorate them with cutouts. For a wipe-clean surface, take your paper place mats to the nearest copy shop and get them laminated.

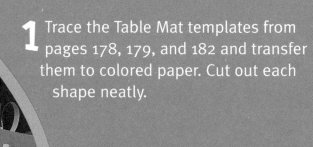

1 Trace the Table Mat templates from pages 178, 179, and 182 and transfer them to colored paper. Cut out each shape neatly.

2 Cut a piece of purple cardboard measuring 12 x 9 in. (30 x 23 cm) and a circle of black paper 8 in. (20.5 cm) in diameter.

3 Stick the black circle to the center of the purple rectangle, then arrange all the other pieces and glue them in place. Cut letters from yellow paper to spell out the names of your dinner guests—to make a personalized place mat for each one!

Hanging Howling Ghosts

Easy and quick to make, hang this fabric ghost where it will take people by surprise—inside a cupboard, perhaps? Or make lots and hang them all around the house. You can use balls of different sizes, cutting the cloth larger or smaller, accordingly.

You will need

Paper pulp ball, 2 in. (5 cm) in diameter	2 pipe cleaners
White fabric	A scrap of black paper
String	Glue stick

1 Thread both ends of a 16 in. (40 cm) length of string through the paper pulp ball. Knot the ends of the string. The ball now hangs from a loop.

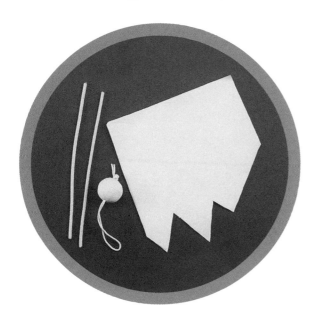

2 Twist the pipe cleaners together and push them in between the two strands of string, above the knot at the base of the ball. These make the ghost's arms.

3 Cut a 24 in. (60 cm) square of white fabric and cut the edges into points. Cut a small hole in the center and push the loop of string through.

4 Tie a length of string around the base of the ball and one around each end of the pipe cleaner arms. Stick on eyes and a mouth cut from black paper.

Ghosts, Ghouls, & Monsters

Do you believe in ghosts and ghouls? Some people do and some people don't. But if you are a believer, Halloween is the time when spirits, gruesome ghouls, and monsters are supposed to be out—so keep a lookout. What is a ghost? When a person passes away, some people think that all the energy leaves the body and enters a new dimension: the paranormal.

People who claim to have "seen" a ghost may have only felt its presence: a cool breeze in an otherwise warm room with the windows and doors shut, perhaps, or a sweet, unexplained scent of roses. Some people just feel that they are being watched when no one is there.

A ghost that can be seen is known as an apparition. This is the kind of ghost that can walk through walls or hover above the ground.

Some ghosts are known as poltergeists. Not only might you see this type of ghost, but you may also be able to hear it wailing or knocking on the walls. Poltergeists are also thought to be able to move things from one place to another.

Don't be afraid...If you hear, see, or smell something strange, it's probably not a ghost! A scratching sound could be mice under the floorboards; strange voices could be your neighbor's TV or radio; a strange vision could just be a shadow from a tree outside or a cloud passing across the sun.

There are lots of scary monsters in books and movies. Two of the most famous are Frankenstein's monster and Count Dracula, the vampire. If you want an original fancy dress costume, or you simply want to conjure up a horrible host of monstrous creatures and terrifying characters to create a petrifying atmosphere on Halloween night, consider these horrors—King Kong, Godzilla, the Hound of the Baskervilles, the headless horseman in Washington Irving's *The Legend of Sleepy Hollow*, Dr. Jekyll and Mr. Hyde, not to mention aliens and terrible sea creatures.

All around the world, people have long believed in different types of ghosts and frightening creatures. Folklore brought these to our imaginations and tradition has kept them alive. Here are just some of them...

✳ **Zombie:** A person believed to have been raised from the grave by a voodoo sorcerer and used to implement evil schemes. Zombies are an accepted phenomenon among some Haitian people, even today.

✳ **Acheri:** An Indian ghost of a small girl. She is believed to bring disease, especially to children, who wear red thread around their necks as protection.

✳ **Domovik:** A spirit that lives behind the stove in Russian myth.

✳ **Afrit:** A vampire-like ghost from Arab mythology.

✳ **Troll:** In Scandinavian folklore, a dwarfish or gigantic creature (either friendly or wicked) who lives in caves and hills.

✳ **Katchinas:** The dead ancestors of Pueblo Native Americans of the United States and Mexico.

✳ **Bogey:** An evil spirit, like a goblin, that likes to scare children.

✳ **Werewolf:** A person who changes into a wolf and eats human flesh or drinks human blood, then reverts to human form. Some African tribes still believe in this phenomenon.

* **Banshee:** From Ireland and Scotland, a female spirit who utters a long, sad cry as a warning that someone is about to die.

* **Kelpie:** From Scottish folklore, a wicked water spirit that will cause you to drown if you see it.

* **Ghoul:** A demon with its origins in Islamic folklore, which feeds on human bodies, living or dead.

* **Kobold:** A mischievous spirit from German folklore.

* **Vampires:** These bloodsucking creatures hail from Eastern European folklore and are said to roam at night, looking to bite the necks of humans and suck their blood. Their victims then also become vampires. Vampires can be warded off with crucifixes, garlic, and sunlight, and they are killed by a stake through the heart or a silver bullet.

* **Puca:** From Irish folklore, these helpful but mischievous spirits can change their shape.

* **Bogart:** From English folklore, this mischievous, goblin-like creature is very disruptive.

* **Demon:** An evil spirit with the power to intervene in people's lives.

* **Bucca:** A sea spirit that helps or hinders Cornish fishermen in England.

Fluttering-Bat Lampshade

If you have a plain lampshade, decorate it with paper cutouts to cast eerie shadows on the walls this Halloween. We have used bats in this project because they cast such a distinctive silhouette, but you could experiment with different shapes if you like.

Trace the bat from page 180 several times onto black construction paper and cut out. The number of bats you need depends on the size of your lampshade. Use tiny pieces of double-sided sticky tape to attach the bats to the inside of the shade, or tiny lumps of sticky tack.

Place the lamp near a blank, light-colored wall where the silhouettes will cast spooky shadows when the light is switched on. You can replace your regular lightbulbs with a colored bulb, available at your local hardware store: experiment with red, blue, and green bulbs to cast an eerie glow.

SAFETY NOTE:
Always get an adult to replace the lightbulb.

Did you know?

One of the reasons bats are linked with Halloween is that long ago people believed witches could change their shape, disguising themselves as animals—and bats were one of the animals they chose to transform themselves into.

Dracula has also become linked with Halloween. This evil character was created by Irish writer Bram (Abraham) Stoker in the nineteenth century. In his story, Dracula is tall and thin with red eyes, pale skin, and pointed fangs. He can change himself into a bat or a wolf, or simply disappear in an evil mist. The fictional Count Dracula may actually be based on a real prince, Vlad Dracula, who ruled in Transylvania 500 years ago and would kill his enemies by driving a sharp stake through their bodies. Dracula's castle may also be based on a real castle in present-day Romania.

The people of Transylvania were afraid of vampires and believed that a corpse would become a vampire if a cat jumped over it before it was buried. They also thought a person would become a vampire if he or she was born with teeth!

In Central and South America there are real vampire bats, with sharp teeth. They drink the blood of horses and cattle but do not attack humans.

Halloween Bunting

These fun decorations can be strung across the ceiling or along the mantelpiece, or even displayed outdoors, as they are reasonably weatherproof.

You will need

White and black posterboard	Pipe cleaners
Craft foam in white, orange, and black	Googly eyes
Pencil	White glue
Scissors	Holepunch

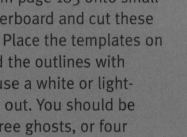
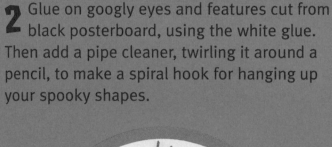

1 Trace the shapes from page 183 onto small pieces of white posterboard and cut these out to make templates. Place the templates on craft foam, draw around the outlines with pencil (on black foam, use a white or light-colored pencil), and cut out. You should be able to get two bats, three ghosts, or four pumpkins from a sheet of foam.

2 Glue on googly eyes and features cut from black posterboard, using the white glue. Then add a pipe cleaner, twirling it around a pencil, to make a spiral hook for hanging up your spooky shapes.

3 Attach each end of a length of string, cord, or ribbon to a curtain pole, or the top of a doorway or window frame (or tree branches if you are using the bunting outdoors). Hook each piece over the string. (If you don't want the shapes to slide up and down the string, squeeze the end of the pipe cleaner so it holds in place.)

Papier Mâché Cauldron

Make a witch's cauldron from papier mâché. With some clever paint effects, you can make it look like metal! Stick it in the middle of the table at Halloween and fill it with goodies!

You will need

A balloon	Cardboard (old cereal boxes are perfect)
Small bowl	Lid from a round jar
White glue	Adhesive tape
Paintbrushes	Acrylic paints in black and
Newspapers	metallic gold or bronze
Paper towels	Wire

1 Blow up a balloon to the size you want your finished cauldron to be and tape it to a bowl, for stability. Mix the glue with an equal volume of water and brush it all over the balloon. Cover it with at least eight layers of newspaper, torn into strips, adding diluted glue with each layer. Leave to dry. Then build up about three more layers, this time using torn strips of paper towel.

2 When the paper is dry, burst the balloon, leaving a thick papier mâché shell. Trim the edge to give a neat bowl shape.

3 Tape the lid to the base of the cauldron, then tape on three rolls of cardboard to make legs. Cover with a few more layers of papier mâché.

4 Paint the cauldron, inside and out, with black paint. Then, using a scrap of paper or cloth, rub the surface with a small amount of metallic gold or bronze paint. Attach a length of wire or string to make a handle.

Papier mâché makes a really hard shell —as long as you add enough layers and as long as the paper is completely soaked in glue. You may find it easier to make the cauldron over a number of days, adding two or three layers of diluted glue and paper each day, and allowing the layers to dry before adding more.

The paper towel, which has an embossed surface, helps to produce a slightly rough effect which, when painted, looks and feels like pitted metal.

Scrumptious Candy Jars

Specially decorated with glass paints, these jars can be filled with sweet treats for Halloween. Simply take an empty jelly jar, wash it thoroughly, and soak off the paper labels. Then get painting! Or you can stick on fake gems using all-purpose glue.

You will need

Sticky tape	Fine paintbrushes
Empty glass jars	Wire
Glass outliner paint, in black	Beads
Water-based glass paints	Pliers

1 Trace your chosen motif onto a scrap of paper and tape the paper inside the jar. Use glass outliner paint to trace the design onto the glass. Leave to dry.

2 Fill in the shapes using colored glass paints. Leave to dry.

3 Cut a length of wire long enough to go twice around the neck of the jar plus three times the desired length of the handle (about one yard [1 m] for an average jar). Start by winding one end once around the neck of the jar, tightly, twisting to fasten.

4 Slip the long end of the wire under the wire around the neck on the opposite side of the jar, to form a handle. Thread the free end with a bead and twist around the handle. Repeat with single beads until you reach the other side of the handle, then thread on a number of beads, enough to go around the neck of the jar, and wind the wire around the neck, twisting the ends of the wire together to fasten. Tuck in the ends.

Make several jars, fill them with candy and arrange them on a sideboard or party table. You could also use these decorated jars as candle holders—but only with strict supervision by an adult. Pour in some sand to form a base for a small candle or tealight.

When buying glass paints, choose the kind that are water-soluble. This means that they contain no harmful solvents and that paintbrushes can be cleaned easily with water and a little soap. Choose transparent (rather than opaque) colors, which look very jewel-like.

Halloween Scrapbook

Fill a special book with Halloween souvenirs and preserve your memories for years to come. Your Halloween scrapbook can include photographs, drawings, cards, menus, invitations, newspaper clippings and pictures from magazines, recipes for party food, jokes, and stories.

You will need

Scrapbook or photo album, 8½ x 11 in. (27.5 x 21 cm)	Glue stick
2 sheets orange paper, 11 x 17 in. (A3)	Scraps of gray, white, black, red, and green paper
2 sheets brown paper, 8½ x 11 in. (A4)	Patterned wrapping paper
Adhesive tape (optional)	Scissors (with wiggly blades, if possible)

1 Cover the front and back covers with orange paper, gluing it in place with a glue stick. Fold the edges of the paper to the inside of each cover, gluing or taping it in place, then cut brown paper to size—about ¼ in. (5 mm) smaller all around than the cover—and glue it on the inside of the cover.

2 Cut out shapes from colored paper—use shapes from page 188 and the template for the haunted house on page 184, or come up with your own designs. Stick each one (except black motifs) onto black paper and cut out, leaving a small border of black, to make each shape stand out.

3 Cut pieces of patterned paper to decorate the inside pages. Use scissors with wiggly blades for a good effect. Back photographs and other memorabilia with paper—use black, white, or a contrasting color, to make it stand out from the background.

If you have a computer, you could produce neat headlines and captions, using a suitably spooky font.

If you prefer not to stick original photographs in your book, get some copies made—reprints, color photocopies, or prints from your computer. You can even produce extras to give to friends and family.

You do not have to use a book exactly the same size and shape as the one described here. Any size will do. Just make sure you choose one with good-quality paper that is strong enough to carry the weight of the items you wish to stick in the scrapbook. The sturdy scrapbook shown here has pages of thick black paper, which makes it ideal.

Captured Spirits

Here is a fun idea to help create a spooky atmosphere in your home at Halloween—tiny "ghosts" trapped in glass jars! They look very effective and are incredibly easy to make. Decide whether you want yours to be a friendly ghost or a nasty one...

You will need

Large glass jar with lid	Glue dots
Translucent fabric (chiffon, thin silk, etc.)	Scrap cardboard or paper
Pen or pencil	String
Scissors	Decorative paper

1 Draw a ghostly shape on the translucent fabric and cut it out. The size of this shape should be about the same height and width as that of the jar.

2 Use glue dots to fix the ghost's hands to the top of the jar, and to fix the top of the head to the inside of the lid.

3 Make labels from scrap paper, write on the name of the spirit— "Wicked Imp," "Evil Banshee" or "Mischievous Sprite," for example—and tie to the neck of the jar. To disguise any printed labels on the jar lid, stick on some decorative paper.

Did you know?

A ghost is the spirit of a dead person that the living believe they can see or hear. And a ghoul is an evil spirit that enters graves and eats the dead bodies within. When the Celts of northern Europe held their festival of Samhain (see page 6), they dressed up as ghosts, hoping to blend in with the real ones that were at large on that night. They would then lead parades to lure all the evil spirits out of town and away from their houses.

Fearsome Finger Puppets

Here is an array of blood-curdling characters: a zombie, a devil, a pumpkin head, a mummy, and a wicked witch. Use your imagination and the same pattern pieces can be adapted to make other characters: a vampire, perhaps, or Frankenstein's monster. Instructions are given for the zombie finger puppet.

For the zombie, you will need

Colored felt: pale blue, white, and beige	Embroidery thread
	Embroidery needle
Paper	Small blue feather
Pencil	Two small buttons
Scissors	

1 Trace the zombie template from page 184 onto a scrap of paper. Pin this to a double layer of pale blue felt and cut out. Do the same with the jacket using beige felt. Cut two small circles of white felt for the eyes.

2 On one of the body pieces, stitch the eyes and the jacket in place. Use dark thread to add details. Stitch the other jacket piece to the remaining body piece, which will form the back of the puppet.

SAFETY NOTE: Children should be supervised by an adult when sewing.

3 Now place the front and back together and sew all around, matching the thread color to the felt. As you stitch the top of the head, insert the feather between the two layers to form hair.

You don't have to be very good at sewing to make a fistful of finger puppets—it just takes a few basic stitches. If, however, you don't like using a needle and thread, use fabric glue instead. Templates for all the other finger puppets are on page 184.

Rainbow Spider's Web

Hang this colorful web on the front door or above the fireplace—adding a big plastic spider and some flies, if you wish. It takes a little time to make but the design is so eye-catching that it's worth the effort.

You will need

Plastic drinking straws	Newspapers or tissue paper
Pipe cleaners	Acrylic paints
Masking tape	Paintbrushes
White glue	Glitter

1 Cut plastic drinking straws into ten 2¼ in. (5.5 cm) lengths, ten 2½ in. (6 cm) lengths, and ten 3 in. (7.5 cm) lengths. Cut ten pipe cleaners into 4 in. (10 cm) lengths.

2 Join the ten shortest straws with lengths of cut pipe cleaner, bending each pipe cleaner in half, like a hairpin, and inserting the ends into two adjacent straws.

3 For the second row, bend a whole pipe cleaner into thirds; push one end through a medium-length straw and into one of the straws in the first row. Insert the other end into a second medium-length straw and through into the next straw in the first row. Take a second pipe cleaner and push one end into the same straw and the other end into a new medium-length straw. Continue until all the medium straws have been used.

4 Make a third row in a similar way to the second row, using the longest straws and whole pipe cleaners.

5 Bind the web with masking tape, to hold the straws and pipe cleaners together, then cover with about three layers of papier mâché. To do this, mix equal quantities of white glue and water, brush over the web, and wind with torn strips of newspaper, tissue paper, or paper towel. Leave to dry.

6 Paint the web white, then use your creativity to decorate it with different colors. Finally, brush with a little white glue and sprinkle with glitter.

Pop-up Party Invitations

Get everyone in the party mood with a wailing ghost or a warty witch's face that really leaps out of the card. Once you've made the invitations, all that's left is to organize a wicked party packed with games—Chapter 5 has some great ideas.

For one ghost invitation, you will need

2 sheets thin black posterboard	Glue
Thin white posterboard	Scissors
Gray paper	Pen and pencil
Yellow paper	Silver pen
Sequin stars	Ruler

1 Fold 2 sheets of black posterboard in half. Take one sheet and cut two slits 2 in. (5 cm) long at right angles to the folded edge, one 3 in. (7.5 cm) up from the bottom, and one 3½ in. (8.5 cm) down from the top. This makes the pop-up section.

3 Cut a wide ghost shape (with a tail!) from a sheet of white card, and fold the tail and right arm as indicated. Stick the left of the ghost to the right-hand side of the pop-up, and the right-hand side of the ghost to the background card.

2 Open out the card, push the pop-up inwards, and close the card again to make creases at the end of the cuts. When you open it out again, the pop-up will form a square. Stick the second sheet of black posterboard to the front of the card to conceal the pop-up.

4 Cut a castle shape from gray paper and stick it to the right-hand side of the card. Add a circle of yellow paper for a moon, and some sequin stars. Write your message on the gray paper, below the castle.

Use the warty witch card in the picture as inspiration for a different type of invitation.

Chapter 4

Food & Drink

Halloween Food

These days it is the custom at Halloween, on both sides of the Atlantic, for children to go trick-or-treating and to collect candy and chocolates. So it may well be that children associate candy with Halloween.

If you are invited to a party at Halloween—or give one yourself—it is likely that you will enjoy a range of Halloween foods such as decorated cookies and the kinds of treats you will find in this chapter. Of course, although these foods may be festive, they are not really "traditional."

Because pumpkin lanterns are such an important part of Halloween, recipes using the scooped-out pumpkin flesh are served by many people at Halloween: pumpkin soup, pumpkin pie, and so on.

Apples, too, are a seasonal fruit firmly linked with Halloween traditions and rituals—so don't be surprised to find apples, or perhaps toffee apples, on the party table or in your trick-or-treat bag.

Cider or ale are often on the menu at this time of year, perhaps with some added spices such as cinnamon, cloves, and nutmeg.

Certain foods are traditionally eaten in different parts of the world on All Saints' Day. In Mexico, for example, they eat Bread of the Dead. In Corsica, they eat *sciacce*, which are small pies filled with mashed potato, garlic,

tomato, and grated cheese. In Sicily, children receive gifts of marzipan fruit, supposedly from the ghosts of their ancestors.

In Ireland, where many of the customs of Halloween began, two traditional foods are used to foretell marriage. Barm brack is a kind of tea bread containing dried fruits; colcannon is a delicious combination of potatoes and collard greens or cabbage. Each dish has a ring buried inside and whoever finds the ring will soon be married.

The Scots enjoy a special variation of oatmeal called crowdie, made with cream, sugar, and rum. Silver charms are hidden in it and each guest takes a spoonful, hoping to recover one of the charms. Each charm has a meaning:

A coin for wealth
A ring for marriage
A button for a bachelor
A thimble for a spinster
A wishbone for your heart's desire

In many parts of Britain, soul cakes are eaten at Halloween (see page 121).

SAFETY WARNING:
The recipes pictured in this chapter often feature plastic props which do not form part of the recipes and which should not be eaten.

Colcannon

1 lb. (450 g) collard greens or cabbage
1 lb. (450 g) potatoes
1 leek, chopped in thin slices
1 cup (225ml) milk

4 oz./½ cup (115 g) butter
Salt and pepper
A pinch of grated nutmeg

1 Place the collard greens or cabbage in a pan of boiling water and cook.

2 Drain the collard greens and leave to cool.

3 Chop the collard greens quite coarsely.

4 Boil the potatoes and mash them with a little of the milk. Season with salt, pepper, and nutmeg.

5 Melt half the butter in a skillet over a medium-low heat, and cook the leeks until soft but not too browned.

6 Add the collard greens and the mashed potatoes to the leeks, mix together, and transfer to a warm serving dish. Make a well in the center and put in the remaining butter.

Did you ever eat colcannon
When 'twas made with
   thickened cream
And the greens and scallions
   blended
Like the picture in a dream?
Did you ever scoop a hole on top
To hold the melting cake
Of clover-flavored butter
That your mother used to make?

(Traditional Irish song)

SAFETY NOTE:
You can bury a ring in the colcannon in the traditional way, but warn your guests so that no one breaks a tooth!

Barm Brack

You will need

1½ pints (850 ml) strong tea (or half strong tea + half Irish whiskey)
1 lb. (450 g) golden raisins
1 lb. (450 g) black raisins
1 lb. (450 g) brown sugar

1 lb. (450 g) all-purpose flour
3 tsp. baking powder
3 eggs
6 tbsp. honey, melted

1 Soak the raisins and sugar in the tea (or tea and whiskey) overnight.

2 Preheat the oven to 300°F (150°C).

3 Add the flour, baking powder, and eggs to the tea mixture.

4 Spoon the dough into greased loaf pans. You should fill 3 loaf pans, 8 x 4 in. (20 x 10 cm).

5 Place the loaf pans in the oven and bake for 1 hour and 45 minutes.

6 Leave the barm brack to cool in the pans for 10 minutes, then turn out onto a cooling rack and glaze the tops with the melted honey.

Soul Cakes

You will need

6 oz. (175 g) butter	A pinch mixed spice
6 oz. (175 g) sugar	2½ oz. (70 g) currants
3 egg yolks	Milk, if necessary
1 lb. (450 g) all-purpose flour, sifted	

1 Preheat the oven to 350°F (180°C) and grease a baking sheet.

2 Cream together the butter and sugar.

3 Beat the egg yolks one at a time into the butter and sugar mixture.

4 Mix in the sifted flour and mixed spice, then fold in the currants. Add a little milk if the dough is too dry.

5 Make 16 balls out of the dough. Place on the baking sheet, leaving at least an inch (2.5 cm) between each ball. Mark each one with a cross. Bake in the oven for 10 to 15 minutes.

Scary Face Pizzas

You will need

1 large margarita pizza	1 oz. (25 g) sweetcorn kernels
A few stuffed olives	1 small carrot
A few pitted black olives	Watercress
1 small red bell pepper	Tomato ketchup in a squeeze bottle

1 Cut out circles from the pizza using a 4 in. (10 cm) cookie cutter, or by cutting around a similar-sized plate. Place the circles on a baking sheet. You will get about 7 circles.

2 Arrange the olives on the pizza circles as eyes. Cut the bell pepper in half and remove the seeds and white pith, then cut into shapes for the mouth. Arrange the sweetcorn kernels for teeth. Cut the carrot into pieces for a nose. Bake according to the cooking instructions on the pizza (you may need to reduce the time a little).

3 Arrange on a platter. Make hair for some of the faces by scattering with watercress or sliced olives, or by squeezing on some ketchup.

Swamp Slime & Ghoul's Eyes

You will need

For the ghouls' eyes	For the swamp slime
4 medium-sized eggs	2 avocados, halved and stone removed
2 tbsp. mayonnaise	6 green onions, finely chopped
8 pitted black olives	1 small handful chopped cilantro
Red food coloring	2 tbsp. red wine vinegar
	2 tbsp. olive oil
	8 fl. oz. (225 ml) sour cream

1 Place the eggs in a pan with enough cold water to cover. Bring to a boil and boil for 7 minutes. Carefully remove from the heat and drain away the hot water. Run under cold water until cool enough to handle.

2 Tap the eggs on a hard surface so that the shells break; peel off the shells. Rinse the eggs under cold water and pat dry. Cut in half and scoop out the egg yolks into a small bowl. Add the mayonnaise and mash with a fork until smooth. Spoon back into the centers of the egg halves and top with an olive to make the eyeball.

3 Dip the end of a toothpick into the red coloring and drag it through the egg yolk mixture to create bloodshot eyes.

4 Place all the ingredients for the swamp slime in a bowl and mash with a potato masher until smooth. Season to taste with salt and freshly ground black pepper. Spoon the swamp slime into a shallow bowl and arrange the ghouls' eyes on top.

Cook's tip

Spread the swamp slime on plates and use two egg halves for eyes, shredded lettuce for hair, sweetcorn kernels for teeth, bell peppers for noses, and black olives for warts—yuk!

Satan's Spicy Salsa

You will need

4 tomatoes, seeds removed and coarsely chopped
1 red onion, peeled and finely chopped
2 cloves garlic, crushed
2 tbsp. olive oil

2 tbsp. tomato ketchup
1 tbsp. lemon juice
Small handful chopped cilantro
Tabasco sauce (optional)

1 Mix together all the ingredients until well combined. Season to taste with salt and freshly ground black pepper. To make it spicy, add a dash of Tabasco sauce—not too much, it really is fiery!

2 Serve with pieces of red and green bell pepper cut into spiky teeth shapes and crackers.

Onion Breath Dip

You will need

4 tbsp. mayonnaise

4 tbsp. creme fraiche

4 tbsp. plain yogurt

3 oz. (75 g) cheddar cheese, grated

4 green onions, trimmed and finely chopped, plus extra to garnish

1 Mix together all the ingredients until well combined. Season to taste with salt and freshly ground black pepper. Spoon into a bowl and garnish with sliced green onion.

2 Serve with sesame seed breadsticks, yellow bell pepper, and green onion.

Spider's Web Dip

You will need

14 oz. (410 g) can chickpeas, drained	2 tbsp. lemon juice
2 cloves garlic, crushed	7 oz. (200 g) tub Greek yogurt
½ tsp. ground cumin	Tabasco sauce (optional)
5 tbsp. tahini	Tomato ketchup in a squeeze bottle

1 Place all the ingredients in a blender with 3–4 tablespoons of water and whizz to a smooth paste. Pour into a bowl and chill for 30 minutes. Season to taste.

2 Carefully squeeze out tomato ketchup to draw a spider's web on the surface of the dip.

3 Serve with potato chips.

Barbecued Bats

To serve 6, you will need

6 tbsp. dark soy sauce	2 tbsp. honey
2 tbsp. tomato ketchup	12 large chicken wings
1 tbsp. Worcestershire sauce	Barbecue sauce and tomato ketchup to serve

1 Mix all the ingredients together and chill overnight or for at least two hours.

2 Turn the broiler to "high." Line a broiler pan with foil shiny side up and arrange the chicken wings on it. Broil for 15–20 minutes, turning regularly, until golden and beginning to char.

3 Arrange two chicken wings on a plate and squirt barbecue sauce in the middle to create a body shape; squirt tomato ketchup for other flying bats. Mayonnaise can be used to create a moon if desired.

Ghoulish Green Pasta

To serve 6, you will need

14 oz. (400 g) black linguine or
tagliatelle verde
4 oz. (100 g) frozen peas

6 tbsp. green pesto sauce
7½ oz. (210 g) can pitted sliced olives
3 tbsp. toasted pine nuts

Cook the pasta in a pan of lightly salted boiling water according to the packet instructions. Add the peas 3 minutes before the end of the cooking time. Drain well. Drain the olives and toss into the remaining ingredients with the pesto sauce and pine nuts, and stir well to combine before serving.

Spooky Sandwiches

Slimy snails

Cut the crusts off a slice of bread and spread with Cheese Whiz or cream cheese. Cut the bread into two strips and roll up like a pinwheel. Cut a thin slice from the length of a gherkin so that it will lie flat. Spread with a little Cheese Whiz or cream cheese and arrange the pinwheel on top to look like a snail. Use a little blob of tomato ketchup for eyes. Or try using your favorite spread—don't go for a spread that is too chunky, as the pinwheel will not stick together.

Empty coffins

Make up your favorite sandwich and cut into a coffin shape by cutting off the two top corners (you can eat those bits now!). Using a sharp knife or a cookie cutter, cut out shapes such as ghosts, angels, stars, and moons, and arrange these around the coffin on a plate.

Monster munch

Make your favorite sandwich filling and use to fill a bread roll. Use two slices of stuffed olives for eyes and fix them to the roll with Cheese Whiz. Cut short, thin strips out of a celery stick and push them into the sides of the roll for legs.

Pumpkin Cauldron Soup

To serve 6, you will need

3 lb. (1.3 kg) pumpkin
1 onion, peeled and chopped
2 garlic cloves
4 tbsp. olive oil

6 baby pumpkins or acorn butternut squash
Finely grated rind and juice of 1 orange
1½ pints (750ml) chicken stock

1 Preheat the oven to 450°F (230°C). Cut the pumpkin in half and scoop out the seeds. Remove the skin and cut the flesh into chunks; scatter in a large roasting pan with the onion and garlic and half the olive oil.

2 Cut a lid off each of the baby pumpkins and scoop out the seeds and discard. (If necessary, cut a small piece of skin from the bottom of each pumpkin so that it stands up straight on a plate). Season the inside of the pumpkins and drizzle with the remaining olive oil. Arrange the pumpkins and lid on a baking sheet and roast alongside the pumpkin chunks for 40 minutes.

3 Turn off the oven. Place the roasted pumpkin chunks in a pan with the orange rind and juice and chicken stock, and bring to a boil. Purée in a blender; season to taste with salt and freshly ground black pepper.

4 Arrange the baby pumpkins on serving plates and fill with the pumpkin soup. Cover each pumpkin with its lid or stand it at the side.

Cook's tip

Eat the soup and then pop a little butter into the shells and scoop out the flesh to eat. Alternatively, make the soup from just the baby pumpkins—roast them, scoop out the flesh and purée it with the roasted onion and garlic, orange rind and juice, and chicken stock.

Bubbling Cauldron Cakes

You will need

1 package orange jello	7 oz. (200 g) confectioners' sugar, sifted
6 chocolate muffins	1 box matchstick chocolates
4 oz./½ cup (100 g) unsalted butter	18 orange jelly snakes
4 tbsp. cocoa powder	Jelly candies including snakes and bottles

1 Make up the jello according to the packet instructions.

2 Peel off the paper cases from the muffins and cut off the tops to level the surface (you can eat the tops).

3 Beat the butter in a bowl until smooth, then stir in the cocoa powder and confectioners' sugar until well combined. Use the mixture to cover the sides of the muffins, making it as smooth as you can.

4 Break the matchstick chocolates in half and arrange in small stacks, together with the orange jelly snakes, to form a fire. Place a muffin—the cauldron—on top.

5 Break up the jello with a fork and spoon it on top of the muffins. Scatter the candies over the jello, pushing them into it. They will look like they are bubbling away in a spooky mixture. The cauldron cakes are ready to serve.

Creepy Chocolate Spiders

You will need

Green food coloring	48 white mini marshmallows
2 oz. (50 g) dehydrated coconut	Prepared frosting in a tube
6 chocolate-covered marshmallow cakes	Candies for the eyes
6 long licorice strips	

1 Mix a few drops of green coloring with the dehydrated coconut to make green grass, stir well to combine, and keep adding a few drops until all the coconut is green.

2 Arrange the green coconut on small side plates. Cut each piece of licorice into strips to make the spider's legs. Pipe a small blob of frosting on the end of each piece and stick 8 pieces to each chocolate marshmallow cake. Stick one mini marshmallow on the end of each leg with the frosting.

3 Fix the eyes in place with a dot of frosting.

Decorated Cookies

For about 20 cookies, you will need

10 oz. (280 g) all-purpose flour	12 oz. (350 g) fondant frosting
7 oz. (200 g) unsalted butter	Prepared frosting in a tube (several colors)
3½ oz. (100 g) confectioners' sugar	Angelica, candies, mini marshmallows etc.
2 egg yolks	(see decorating ideas below)
1 tsp. vanilla extract	

1 Preheat the oven to 400°F (200°C). Lightly grease two baking sheets.

2 Place the flour, butter, and confectioners' sugar into a food processor and blend to make fine "bread crumbs." Add the egg yolks and vanilla extract and blend to a firm dough. Wrap in plastic wrap and chill for 30 minutes.

3 Roll out the dough on a lightly floured work surface until it is ¼ in. (5 mm) thick. Cut out about twenty 3 in. (7.5 cm) fluted or plain circles using a cookie cutter. Transfer to the baking sheets and bake for 8–10 minutes until golden brown. Let cool for 5 minutes before transferring them to a cooling rack to cool completely.

4 Roll out the fondant frosting and cut out twenty plain circles just a little smaller than the cookies. Dot the cookies with frosting from the tube and cover with the circle of rolled out frosting. Press down gently to secure. Now you can begin to make the faces.

Pumpkins
Color the fondant frosting orange with paste food coloring (liquid will make it too soft). Use a tube of black frosting to create the eyes, nose, and mouth. Use angelica, cut into shapes, for the stalk and leaves.

Spooky faces
Use mini Smarties or candies for eyes, noses, and mouths, and a tube of frosting to make warts, scars, or spots—red and yellow are good for this!

Slimy Swamp Bugs

You will need

1 packet lime jello   jelly snake candies

Make up the jello according to the instructions and chill until set. Break up with a fork and mix with the jelly candies. Spoon into a shallow bowl. Serve with a squirt can of whipped cream.

Chocolate Web Desserts

You will need

1 packet lime jello   3 oz. (75 g) semisweet chocolate

1 Make up the jello according to the instructions, pour into 4 glasses, and leave to set in the refrigerator. (Alternatively, you could use different flavors of jello.)

2 Break the chocolate into small pieces and place in a bowl. Stand over a small pan of simmering water until melted. Turn off the heat and carefully lift away from the pan with oven mitts.

3 Line a baking tray with wax paper. If you don't already have one, make a plastic piping bag by opening a small plastic sandwich bag and placing it in a cup, allowing any excess to hang over the edge. Carefully pour in the chocolate. Lift out the bag and twist to enclose the chocolate at one end. Carefully snip a small piece off the corner. Now pipe two crosses, about 2 in. (5 cm) across, on top of each other, as shown in the photo. Then pipe a curved line between each straight line to create a web design. Allow to cool completely.

4 Using a round-bladed knife, carefully lift the web from the paper. If you like, squirt some cream on the dessert before placing the web.

Pumpkin Truffles

For 16 truffles, you will need

4 oz. (100 g) plain chocolate
3 oz. (75 g) Madeira cake crumbs
3 oz. (75 g) confectioners' sugar
4oz. (100 g) ground almonds
2 tbsp. sherry or fresh orange juice

2 tbsp. heavy cream
3 oz. (75 g) dried mixed fruit
1 lb. (450 g) orange fondant frosting
4 oz. (100 g) green fondant frosting

1 Melt the chocolate in a bowl set over a pan of simmering water. Let cool slightly, then stir in the cake crumbs, confectioners' sugar, ground almonds, sherry or orange juice, cream, and mixed fruit. Stir until well combined. Chill for 30 minutes.

2 Divide the green frosting into 16 equal-sized balls. Flatten slightly and pinch a little stalk in the center of each flattened piece. Cut out leaf shapes around the flattened piece to create the calyx for the top of each pumpkin. Score each leaf with the tip of a sharp knife for the leaf's veins.

3 Roll out the orange frosting on a surface lightly dusted with confectioners' sugar until it is ⅛ in. (3 mm) thick. Cut out sixteen circles measuring 3½ in. (9 cm) in diameter.

4 Divide the truffle mixture into 16 equal-sized balls and wrap an orange frosting circle around each one, pinching the fondant up around the top of the truffle. Using the tip of a sharp knife, cut out the eyes and mouth. Brush the base of each calyx with a little water to help it stick, and position on the top of the pumpkin heads.

Skeleton Popsicles

For 24 popsicles, you will need

6 oz. (175 g) butter	A little milk
6 oz. (175 g) superfine sugar	12 oz. (350 g) white fondant frosting
1 medium egg, beaten	24 flat wooden popsicle sticks
12 oz. (350 g) all-purpose flour	6 oz. (175 g) bittersweet chocolate
1 tsp. baking powder	Black food coloring
1 tsp. mixed spice	

1 Preheat the oven to 350°F (180°C). Cream the butter and sugar together until pale, beat in the egg and stir in the flour, baking powder, and mixed spice. If necessary, add a little milk to bind to a soft, pliable dough. Chill for 30 minutes.

2 Roll out the dough on a lightly floured surface until it is ¼ in. (5 mm) thick. Cut out 24 circles, 4 in. (10 cm) in diameter, with a round cutter. Arrange the circles on two baking sheets, slip a popsicle stick 1 in. (2.5 cm) under each cookie, and press down lightly. Bake for 10–12 minutes until pale golden. Cool on the baking sheets for 10 minutes before transferring to a cooling rack to cool completely.

3 Roll out the frosting on a surface lightly dusted with confectioners' sugar until it is ⅛ in. (3 mm) thick. Make a paper template of a skull and cut out 24 skull shapes (roll out the frosting again).

4 Melt the chocolate in a bowl set over a pan of simmering water. Spoon into a paper piping bag and snip off the tip. If necessary, secure the popsicle sticks to the cookies with some of the melted chocolate and let it set. Pipe small dots over the top half of the cookies and arrange the skulls on top. Pipe eyes and a nose on each of the skulls. Paint on the mouth and teeth with black food coloring.

Toothy Bites

To make 8, you will need

8 Wagon Wheel cookies	7 oz. (200 g) bag mini white
8 scoops of your favorite ice cream	marshmallows

1 Cut each Wagon Wheel cookie in half and sandwich the halves together with a scoop of ice cream. Pinch the halves together at one side to give you an open mouth shape. Freeze for 20 minutes.

2 Cut the mini marshmallows in half lengthwise and push into the ice cream to make teeth.

Muddy Worm Sundae

To serve 4, you will need

2 chocolate chip muffins	10 fl. oz. (300 ml) heavy cream
2 bananas, peeled and sliced	Grated chocolate and jelly worms
8 tbsp. toffee sauce	

1 Break up the chocolate muffins and arrange in the base of four glasses. Top with half the bananas. Drizzle with one tablespoon of toffee sauce and scatter a few jelly worms on top.

2 Whip the cream and spoon into the glasses. Top with the remaining bananas and worms and drizzle with the rest of the toffee sauce. Scatter with grated chocolate and serve immediately.

Meringue Ghosts

You will need

2 egg whites
4½ oz. (125 g) superfine sugar
1 oz. (25 g) semisweet chocolate

Prepared frosting in a tube (glitter)
Candies to serve

1 Turn the oven on to 275°F (140°C). Draw six spooky ghost shapes (trace the template on this page) on wax paper and turn the paper over onto a baking sheet.

2 Place the egg whites in a large, clean bowl and beat with an electric mixer until thick and glossy. Slowly sprinkle in the sugar and beat until well combined (add the sugar little by little, mixing well each time, until all the sugar has been used).

3 Spoon the mixture equally into the ghost shapes and spread it to fit. Place in the oven for 1 hour until crisp and dry. Turn off the heat and open the oven door slightly; let cool completely in the oven.

4 Carefully remove the meringue ghosts from the paper and place on a dark plate. Break the chocolate into small pieces and place in a bowl. Stand over a small pan of simmering water until melted. Pour the chocolate into a paper piping bag, if you have one. If not, pour the chocolate into a plastic sandwich bag and snip one corner of the bag to create a piping bag. Pipe eyes and spooky screaming mouths on the meringue ghosts. Use the glitter frosting to pipe "Oooooooo!" on the plate before serving. Decorate with candies.

Cook's tip

Look out for frosting in a tube—it is the ideal substance for sticking candies to cookies and cakes. It also comes in a glitter gel form which is totally edible and will add to the magical effect.

Witches' Fingers

For about 40 fingers, you will need

For the fingers	
4½ oz. (125 g) softened butter	40 whole blanched almonds
4½ oz. (125 g) confectioners' sugar	Prepared frosting in a tube (red)
1 small egg, beaten	For the chocolate dip
1 tsp. almond extract	6 tbsp. chocolate hazelnut spread
9 oz. (250 g) all-purpose flour	½ pint (300ml) heavy cream
1 tsp. baking powder	
1 tsp. salt	

1 Heat the oven to 325°F (160°C).

2 Beat the butter in a large bowl until creamy. Sift in the sugar, add the egg and almond extract, and mix well. Stir in the flour, baking powder, and salt until the mixture forms a firm dough. Wrap in plastic wrap and chill for at least 30 minutes.

3 Break the dough into 40 pieces and shape into skinny fingers about 3 in. (7.5 cm). Place on a baking sheet and press a whole almond into one end of each finger.

Bake the fingers for 15–20 minutes until golden. Remove from the oven carefully and let cool.

4 Squeeze a little red frosting from the tube onto each almond and spread it with a clean, wet pastry brush.

5 Beat the chocolate spread with half the cream until smooth and thick. Whip the remaining cream and fold through to create a marbled effect. Spoon into a bowl. To serve, arrange the fingers around the bowl.

Wicked Witches' Hats

To make 8 hats, you will need

8 wafer ice cream cones	8 graham crackers
3 oz. (75g) soft margarine	8 oz. (225 g) graham crackers, crushed
2 tbsp. chocolate powder	4½ oz. (125g) golden raisins
2 tbsp. superfine sugar	Prepared frosting in a tube
1 tbsp. corn syrup	7 oz. (200 g) semisweet melted chocolate
	A tube of mini Smarties or candies

1 Very carefully cut the open, wide half off each wafer cone, leaving a smaller cone to make the top of each hat.

2 Melt the margarine, chocolate powder, superfine sugar, and corn syrup in a pan. Stir until the sugar has dissolved. Stir in the graham crackers and golden raisins and stir well to combine. Let cool slightly. Then spoon into the wafer cones.

3 Pipe some frosting around the top of the wafer cone and then stick a graham cracker on the end to create the hat shape. Repeat until you have eight hat shapes. Place on a cooling rack standing over a baking sheet.

4 Break the chocolate into small pieces and place in a bowl. Stand over a small pan of simmering water until melted. Using oven mitts, carefully lift the bowl off the pan. Spoon the chocolate over the hats to cover completely. (You may need to re-melt the drips caught in the baking sheet beneath.) Let cool completely.

5 Decorate the hats by sticking on candies with a small dot of frosting.

Toffee Apples

For 6 apples, you will need

6 medium sized apples	2 tsp. white wine vinegar
6 wooden popsicle sticks	1/4 pint (150 ml) water
1 lb. (450 g) unrefined brown sugar	1 tbsp. corn syrup
2 oz. (50 g) butter	

1 Lightly butter a baking sheet. Wipe the apples with a clean, damp cloth and push a popsicle stick into the core of each one.

2 Place all the remaining ingredients in a large, heavy-based pan and cook, stirring occasionally, until all the sugar has dissolved. Bring to a boil and boil rapidly for about five minutes.

SAFETY NOTE:
Melted sugar gets extremely hot and can be dangerous; therefore, only adults should make this recipe.

3 Remove the pan from the heat. Dip each apple in the syrup to cover, lift up out of the toffee syrup and let any excess drip away. Place on the baking sheet and leave until the toffee is hard and cool before serving. Make and eat on the same day. While the toffee is still soft, the apple can also be dipped into candy shots, chopped mixed nuts, other small candies.

After you have coated all the apples, combine the remaining toffee with chopped mixed nuts, M&Ms, chocolate chips, or other small candies to make tasty little rollups of fun!

Really Revolting Drinks

Witches' Brew

To serve 6 people, you will need

10 fl. oz. (300 ml) each cranberry juice, ginger ale, and orange juice

Blue and green food coloring

Mix together the cranberry juice, ginger ale, and orange juice until well combined. Stir in the food coloring until you have a disgusting-looking grayish-green drink.

Love Potion

To serve 6, you will need

6 scoops vanilla ice cream
1½ pints (900 ml) lemon-lime soda
Whipped cream
Candy shots

Place a scoop of ice cream in a drinking glass. Pour the soda over it (the ice cream will float to the surface). Top with cream and decorate with candy shots.

Banana Sludge

To serve 4–6, you will need

3 large bananas
12 scoops vanilla ice cream
Fresh lemon juice
Chocolate sauce

Mix the bananas, vanilla ice cream, and lemon juice in a blender (or mash by hand) until smooth. Drizzle chocolate sauce on the sides of drinking glasses, then pour in the banana sludge. Top with more chocolate sauce and serve immediately.

Chapter 5

Games &
Tricks

Games with Apples

Apples have an important role to play in pagan lore. Long ago, in Britain, apples were used in fertility rites. In the apple bobbing ritual, the bowl of water was said to represent the cauldron of rebirth. In Cornwall, children would be given apples on All Hallows' Eve as a symbol of long life.

Bobbing for apples

Bobbing for apples is an ancient game—and a wet one! Here's what you need to do. Fill a large container with water and add as many apples as you like; they will float on the surface. The object of the game is to get hold of one of the apples and remove it from the water using only your mouth—no cheating! To make the game more difficult, the apples' stems should be removed.

It is a good idea to cover the floor with plastic sheeting—unless you are playing outdoors—and to make "trash bag overalls" for the participants: just cut a hole in the bottom of a plastic trash bag and, for a festive touch, decorate with stuck-on stars.

According to tradition, each (unmarried) participant made a tiny mark on an apple to identify it as his or her own. Then everyone placed their apples and a few unmarked ones in the water, and attempted to bite one of the floating apples. Whoever owned the apple that a participant succeeded in biting was destined to be that person's future husband or wife.

Did you know?

Young people used apples to try to predict who—or if—they would marry, or to discover if a lover was faithful. If you want to discover the name of your future husband or wife, try this: peel an apple in one long continuous strip, then allow the peel to fall on the floor, where it will form his or her initials.

Alternative apple bobbing

This is a lively game guaranteed to get your Halloween off to a great start. Tie lengths of string to the stems of several apples and suspend them from a length of rope. Two players hold the ends of the rope while others try to take bites from the apples without using their hands. Or tie the rope to a beam, a door frame, or a washing line.

Instead of the traditional apples, you could suspend ring doughnuts and watch all the players end up with sugary faces as they attempt to take big bites out of them. You could also use pretzels, marshmallows, or other edible treats.

Other ideas

Pass the apple

Line up players in teams and give the first person in each team an apple to place under his or her chin. The object of the game is to pass the apple to the next person in line without using your hands. The first team to pass the apple all the way to the last person is the winner. If anyone drops the apple, the team has to start again.

Dig for treasure

For a very messy and lively party game, fill a large plastic bowl or bucket with cooked spaghetti or jello, or something else that is very squishy. Bury wrapped candy and other treats inside. Blindfold players and let them plunge their hands deep into the gunk in order to retrieve one of the treats.

Fortune-telling

Pretend you are a fortune-teller and ask your friends to come to you to have their fortunes told. Tell them to think of some good questions that they have been dying to know the answer to.

Dress as a fortune-teller. You will need to tie a scarf around your head, and put on some gold earrings. Girls can wear a full skirt, with a blouse and a shawl; boys can wear pants with a loose white shirt, a waistcoat, and a colorful sash.

1 You will need a crystal ball. The real thing is very expensive, so improvise with an upturned glass bowl.

2 Make a set of fortune-telling cards. Cut out small rectangles of card and write a prediction on each. These should be general answers, such as "Wait and see," "You will be lucky," "Not this time," or "The future is in your own hands."

3 Spread out the cards. When your "clients" consult you and ask questions—such as "Will I pass my exams?" "Will my missing cat ever be found?" or "Does that cute boy in my class even know I exist?"—ask them to choose a card, and read out the prediction in a dark and mysterious voice.

Other ideas

Instead of writing predictions on cards, fill a notebook with "answers" and vague predictions, one to a page. When someone asks you a question, open the book at random to read your reply. The way you interpret what is written on the page in relation to the question is up to you—you are the fortune-teller! Predictions could be: "You will achieve success," "You will need assistance," "Don't be afraid," "Follow your heart," "Think again," "Trust your instincts," "Don't be foolish," "No one can tell," and so on.

Ancient fortune-telling rituals

Good luck charm

Throw a stone into the fire and make a wish. When the fire goes out and the ashes are completely cold—you'll have to wait until the following day—retrieve the stone and keep it safe, and you'll have good fortune throughout the coming year. If you can't find your stone in the ashes, however, it means bad luck.

What does the future hold?

Throw nuts—preferably hazelnuts, which were sacred to the ancient Celts—on the fire to determine your fortune for the year ahead. If a nut burns brightly, for example, you will have good health. If it flares up with a sudden bright light, you will get married!

Finding a lover

Throw two nuts on a fire. Give each the names of a potential lover. The one that cracks first will be the one for you!

Will I be rich or poor?

Place three bowls together; leave one empty, fill one with clean water, and one with dirty water. Each person should be blindfolded and led to the bowls in turn, and asked to touch one. This indicates their fate—the clean water predicts marriage to a rich person; the dirty water that he or she will marry a poor person; and the empty bowl indicates no marriage at all.

SAFETY NOTE:
Some of these fortune-telling rituals involve fire and can therefore be dangerous. Make sure that all children are supervised by an adult when playing these games.

Haunted House

If you are having guests over at Halloween, why not turn your house into a haunted castle, then take them on a guided tour...Use props, sound effects, and trickery to create a real-life haunted house that will have your guests running screaming from the room!

You could escort your guests, or you could let them wander through the house alone while you hide behind doors or curtains adding sound effects—wobble a large sheet of cardboard or bang a metal baking sheet for thunder, flap a plastic bag to mimic flying bats, pour uncooked rice onto a baking sheet to sound like rain, and so on. A microphone and a hidden speaker will amplify spooky whispers and groans.

To transform your house, use any or all of the following ideas, depending on what your house is like. Start with the entrance—the front path, steps, porch, or front door—then work your evil way through the house, fixing up every room your guests are likely to visit. Some of the ideas will be noticed by everyone but some are more subtle and will be noticed by only your most observant guests.

Starting at the front door, put up a sign saying "Enter at your peril" or something equally offputting. Make a scarecrow to stand in the garden, using a broomstick with a head made from an old sack stuffed with straw. Tie a stick across the upright broomstick to create arms and add old clothes stuffed with straw or crumpled plastic bags.

Stick windmills in the flower beds or window boxes outside your house and they will whirr and rattle when the wind catches them. Or make some Halloween wind chimes by tying various objects—old silverware, bones, sticks, bits of broken jewelry, and bottle tops—onto strong thread and hang several of these together, so the objects bump and clatter into each other in the breeze.

In the entrance hall or foyer, have some spooky music playing. You could record your own soundtrack of music overlaid with groans and screeches. If you have any family portraits on the walls, stick on false beards and glasses, or give them evil expressions (make sure these can be removed afterward without causing any damage).

In the dining room, set up a moldy fruit bowl. Spray plastic fruit black, adding patches of green "mold" by rubbing on some green eyeshadow or dabbing with glue and sprinkling with flour. Add a few rubber worms, embedded among the fruits.

Wind lengths of real or fake ivy around chair backs, table legs, and other furniture for a look of neglect. Arrange waxy white lilies, real or fake, in a tall vase, or use dead roses.

Buy fake cobwebs from a party store to hang from the corners of the room. Suspend plastic spiders on lengths of invisible thread from ceiling, door frames, and lampshades.

In the living room, have a spooky movie playing on the video or DVD player (check with your parents that what you are viewing has an appropriate rating). Turn out all the lights…

For further effect, hang glow-in-the-dark bats from the ceiling and watch what happens when you turn out the lights!

In the kitchen, make paper labels for the cans and jars in the food cupboard: transform cans of spaghetti into "worms" and cat food into "shredded mice." Use your imagination.

Put bugs in the fridge: buy edible gummy worms and other creatures from the grocery store and place them on the cheese, around the neck of the milk jug—everywhere!

In the bedroom, create a crime scene on the carpet. Lie on the floor and get someone to draw around your body with white chalk, or use white electrical tape.

Another idea is to leave a "dead body" lying around. Stuff old clothes—a pair of pants and a shirt—with newspapers and place them on the floor or bed in a curled-up position. Add a hat, shoes, and gloves for further realism. You could stick a knife in the chest, adding a squirt of red paint or fake blood (but only if it is an old shirt).

In the bathroom, spread some chips or cornflakes under a rug. When people walk over it, they will be surprised by the crunching sounds underfoot.

Place a false hand (from a party store) behind the toilet. Or have a pair of shoes poking out from under the shower curtain. In fact, if you are allowed to, you could spatter the bath or shower with fake blood for a really gruesome effect!

You could also buy or rent a lifesize rubber skeleton from a party store and hang it in the shower or closet.

All over the house, put plastic rats, spiders, and snakes (from a toy store or party store) in corners, under tables, on shelves—all over the place. When the lights are dim, they look quite real!

For a cobwebby effect that will give your whole house an abandoned appearance, pull cotton batting apart, creating spidery threads, and drape these over furniture and across doorways.

Cover the walls temporarily with dark-colored paper or lengths of fabric in black, deep red, navy blue, or bottle green.

Soft lighting or shaded lamps will lower the light levels and cast long shadows. Replace your regular lightbulbs with colored bulbs—red, blue, and green—from the local hardware store, to cast an eerie glow.

If your curtains or blinds don't block out enough light, cover the windows with blankets, black trash bags, or aluminum foil to block it out completely.

Bear in mind that, when your house is dark or dimly lit, it's a good idea to have some reflective tape over the doorways so people can easily find their way out.

Ghostly Games

Are you having a party this Halloween? Here are some games with a festive theme, to suit all ages. They can easily be played at home but some need preparation, so before your party starts, think about which games you want to play and make sure everything is ready in advance.

Guess the weight of the pumpkin

Choose a nice big pumpkin—but not so large that people can't pick it up. Let each person in turn hold the pumpkin and try to guess its weight. After everyone has had a turn, weigh the pumpkin using a bathroom scale. The person who guessed nearest to the correct weight wins a prize.

Ghostly guessing game

Everyone stands in a circle. Blindfold one player, who stands in the center and spins around. When he or she stops, the person facing him or her should say, "Whoooooo am I?" The blindfolded person must guess and, if correct, that person puts on the blindfold and the game continues.

Musical graves

Cut gravestones from large rectangles of paper and place them on the floor. There should be one fewer gravestone than there are people playing the game. Play some spooky music and, instead of dancing, everyone walks around the room like the undead. When the music stops, each person lies down on a gravestone. The person who fails to find a grave to lie on is out. Remove one gravestone and let the game continue. The game finishes when there are two people competing for a single grave and the winner is the one who manages to get to it first.

Vampire kiss chase

A variation on a classic playground game, the person who is the "vampire" chases the others and, when they are caught, instead of kissing them, pretends to bite them on the neck. Bitten victims then become vampires too and chase the others until everyone has become a vampire.

Flying bats

Cut out large bat shapes from black tissue paper. (Enlarge the template from page 178.) Give each player a paper bat and a straw. The aim is to keep the bat afloat by blowing through the straw.

The murder game

Cut out small squares of paper. On one of them, write the word "murderer" and leave all the others blank. Players stand in a circle and remain silent. Hand each person a piece of paper. The murderer has to wink at each of the other people without anyone else noticing. Anyone who is winked at is dead. Players have to guess who the murderer is before he or she can wink at them.

Shadow Play

Turn out all the lights except one and use it to create shadows on a blank wall. You could even make a few shadow puppets to illustrate your very own ghost story.

1 Make a shadow puppet by tracing the shapes from pages 185–186 onto black cardboard.

2 Punch holes where indicated and attach arms and legs using brads. The brads will allow you to move the arms, legs, and head into different positions.

3 Tape a stick to the body of the witch. Using a desk lamp pointed at a blank wall or large sheet of paper, make spooky shadows with the puppet.

You could also make shadows with your hands, holding them close to the light source to create a really crisp shadow on the wall or screen. Try making a ghost shape, a werewolf, a bat, or any others than come to mind.

Spooky stories

The telling of ghost stories has, for years, been a widespread pastime at Halloween. Get some friends together and tell a few of your own. If there is a group of people, tell a story together. With the lights dimmed, one person should start the story and speak for one minute, then the next person takes over. Each person adds to the story until it reaches a scary conclusion. You could pass around a flashlight and let the person who is the storyteller hold it under his or her chin—try it and see how scary you look.

Eerie noises

While spooky stories are being told, why not add some sound effects? It's even more effective if you can borrow a microphone, which will amplify spooky whispers and groans.

* For thunder, wobble a large sheet of cardboard or a metal baking sheet.

* For the sound of flying bats or other flapping wings, flap a plastic bag.

* For rain, pour uncooked rice onto a baking sheet.

Touchy-feely

This is not for the fainthearted! Fill plastic containers such as clean, empty margarine tubs with a variety of items. Fill one with peeled grapes, another with cooked spaghetti, another with rice, and another with an apple with holes cut out for mouth, nose, and eyes.

Now sit your friends in a circle, blindfolded, while you tell them a scary story. As you recount the gruesome details, pass around the bowls, encouraging them to feel the contents. Try to include some maggots in the story and, as you do, pass around the bowl of rice; as you mention eyeballs, pass around the grapes, and so on. Make up your own stories depending on what you have available—clean chicken bones for human bones, pumpkin seeds for bats' toenails—and let your imagination run wild!

Halloween Memory Game

Staying up until the witching hour? Pass the time with a friend or two, playing this engrossing game. It's a well-known memory game but it has been customized to make it ideal for Halloween.

You will need

Cardboard (mounting board)	Glue stick
Craft knife	Box
Steel ruler	Colored paper

1 You are going to need a number of pictures—two copies of each. You could use giftwrap with a repeating pattern, or copy pictures from page 188, or from another source.

2 Cut out each picture and stick it onto the cardboard to make playing cards. Cut them into neat rectangles with the craft knife and steel ruler. Each card should measure exactly the same size—2⅝ x 2⅞ in. (6.5 x 7 cm).

3 Keep all the playing cards in a box and decorate the lid with paper cutouts traced from the cover of this book.

How to play

Place all the cards face down on a flat surface, either in a random pattern or in neat rows. Players take turns to select two cards and turn them face up so everyone can see. If the two cards match, the player keeps them and takes another turn. If not, they are placed face down again and the next player has a turn. The winner is the one with the most matching pairs when all the cards have gone.

More Memory Games

Here are two more fun Halloween games that are suitable for all ages. They can be played toward the end of a Halloween party when you all just want to sit down for a while and play a quiet game.

The tray of doom

You will need paper and pencils, a tray, a cloth, and a number of weird and wonderful objects with a Halloween theme.

Arrange the items on the tray and let the players look at it for exactly one minute. Then cover it up with the cloth. The object of the game is to see how many items people can remember. The person who writes down all the items—or the highest number— wins a prize. Suitable items might include plastic toys, a lock of hair, an apple or small pumpkin, a candle, and so on. For older players, you could arrange up to twenty items; for younger ones, make it a lot fewer.

Creepy castle

This game requires no equipment. Just get everyone gathered around and sitting comfortably and you're ready to begin.

The first player starts by saying something like, "I went to the creepy castle and I saw a wicked witch." The next person repeats this and adds something else: "I went to the creepy castle and I saw a wicked witch and an ugly troll." The next person repeats the whole thing and adds his or her own contribution at the end. Continue like this, with players being forced to drop out of the game if they forget one of the items. The game grinds to a halt when there are too many things for anyone to remember.

Trick-Or-Treating Origins

You might think that "trick-or-treating"—where children dress up at Halloween and knock on neighbors' doors threatening to play a trick if they are not given a treat—is a modern custom. But you'd be wrong.

Trick-or-treating has its origins in ancient British customs. It was once the practice in Ireland for people to go door to door, collecting money, bread, cakes, nuts, and apples in preparation for the harvest festival. They would also beg for soul cakes (see the recipe on page 121) in exchange for blessings and promises of prosperity, or protection against bad luck. If the residents of the houses refused to supply them with soul cakes—or other treats such as fruit, sweets, or money—they would play a practical joke on them. Does that sound familiar?

Irish people believed that fairies were around on the night of Halloween, and many people would leave an offering of food or milk on the doorstep in the hope that the occupants would be blessed by the fairies—whom they called the "good folk"—throughout the following year.

Both the Irish and the Scots also had their Halloween "night of mischief" when the boys of the area would join together and visit neighborhood houses, causing a disturbance, expecting the householders to bribe them with treats to make them go away. While the boys were out playing pranks and causing mischief,

the girls would stay indoors, performing rituals to forecast their marriage prospects. Meanwhile, the older people would blame all the chaos and mayhem on the fact that the spirits were abroad that night.

In the nineteenth century, many Irish and Scottish people emigrated to America and brought their customs and rituals with them.

In New York, in the middle of the nineteenth century, children called "ragamuffins" would dress in costumes and beg for pennies from adults on Thanksgiving Day. In the Depression years of the 1930s, there were far more people begging on the streets at Thanksgiving and some of the tricks became more menacing. The authorities in the towns and cities tried to limit the practice of using threatening behavior to demand money or food and began to organize "safe" Halloween events, where householders would hand out bribes to the neighborhood children. The ragamuffins either stopped their Thanksgiving begging or began to do it at Halloween instead.

These days, Halloween is such a big event in the U.S.A. and the U.K. that it has become big business. Shops begin selling merchandise weeks beforehand, and on the night itself, there are throngs of children in costume knocking on doors in the hope of collecting some treats. Households that approve of trick-or-treaters tend to put up some kind of display—a wreath on the door, fairy lights, jack-o'-lanterns, or the like—so that children know they will receive a good welcome. It is probably wise to avoid homes that are not decorated. In fact, many householders see trick-or-treaters as a threat—and is it any wonder when some children think it's amusing to throw eggs at doors and windows,

or believe that Halloween gives them an excuse for antisocial behavior?

If you are going out trick-or-treating, try to be considerate to people who do not wish to participate. The tricks you choose to perform should not cause harm to people or pets. or damage to property. Similarly, if you are at home on All Hallows' Eve, and wish to enter into the festive spirit, why not be prepared with a dish of candy, a bowl of apples, or a pile of loose change to offer any trick-or-treaters who come knocking on your door?

Goblins On A Rampage
© Wooster Scott

Trick-Or-Treat Sacks

A few days before Halloween, make up some decorated sacks for friends you have invited to your home—or for yourself, to collect goodies when you go out trick-or-treating. There are lots of Halloween designs to choose from: try a bat or a pumpkin motif using the templates on page 178.

You will need

Burlap, 21 x 10½ in. (52 x 26 cm)	Embroidery thread in matching colors
	Sewing thread
Felt in white, black, and orange	String or cord

1 Trace the witch silhouette from the front cover of this book and cut out the shape from black felt. Cut a 5¼ x 3¼ in. (13 x 8 cm) rectangle of dark orange felt and a circle of white felt 3 in. (7.5 cm) in diameter.

2 Fold the burlap in half and position the felt shapes on one side. Pin, then stitch in place using embroidery thread to match the color of the piece you are stitching.

3 With the right sides together, sew up the sides of the bag. Turn right side out. Turn under ⅝ in. (1.5 cm) along the top of the bag and stitch in place. Cut two 8 in. (20 cm) lengths of string, poke through the fabric, and knot in place to form handles.

At dinnertime on Halloween, put a trick-or-treat bag at each place setting, filled with candy or small gifts. Even if you are not having a party, it will create a festive atmosphere.

Even if your sewing skills are pretty basic, this bag is easy to make. Instead of burlap, you could use fleece and felt, which do not fray and are therefore easy to stitch. Instead of the witch, you could cut your own bold Halloween shapes from felt and, instead of stitching them in place, you could stick them on using fabric glue.

Trick-Or-Treat Bags

You'll need to know how to sew a little to make these bags, so if you are not very confident using a needle and thread, get an adult to show you how to do some basic stitches and make sure they supervise you while you do it. But don't worry, using Bondaweb makes these bags very simple to make!

You will need

Black cotton fabric 17½ x 7¼ in. (44 x 18 cm)	Pencil
Bondaweb	Orange, white, and yellow fabric.
	Needle and thread

1 Using the templates on page 187, trace a skull and crossbones or a pumpkin face, using a pencil, directly onto the paper backing of the Bondaweb. Cut out roughly, leaving a margin of about ⅝ in. (1.5 cm) all around each motif.

2 Place the Bondaweb motifs, paper side up, on the fabric—white for the skull and orange for the pumpkin. Fuse the Bondaweb to the fabric using a hot iron and following the manufacturer's instructions. Cut out around the pencil lines.

3 Peel off the backing paper and apply your motif to one half of the black fabric, fixing it in place using the hot iron. This will form the front of your bag.

4 Hem the short sides of the black fabric. You can do this by folding over ⅝ in. (1.5 cm) to the inside and stitching; or cut a ⅝ in. (1.5 cm) strip of Bondaweb, apply it to the edge using the hot iron, fold over to the inside, and press with the iron again to fix. Then fold the fabric in half, with the right sides together and sew up the two sides to make a bag.

5 Make handles from a strip of contrasting fabric, 20 x 2 in. (50 x 5 cm). With the right sides together, fold this strip in half lengthwise and stitch ¼ in. (5 mm) from the long edge. Turn right side out and cut in half, then attach one strip to each side of the bag. Turn the bag right side out. To close the bag, tie the handles together.

Trick-Or-Treat Bucket

Next time you go to the movies, save your popcorn bucket—it makes a great container for collecting Halloween treats. This project uses the papier mâché technique (like in the Papier Mâché Cauldron on page 100 and the Papier Mâché Pumpkin on page 72) so you'll soon be an expert!

You will need

Popcorn bucket | Paintbrush
White glue | Ribbon or cord
Tissue paper | White or silver glitter
Acrylic paints in black and red

1 See the instructions for making papier mâché on page 100. Cover the popcorn bucket with several layers of papier mâché, to strengthen it and give a good surface for painting.

2 Leave it to dry before painting the outside black and the inside red. When the paint is dry, decorate with a spider's web, using undiluted white glue, sprinkled with glitter.

Spells & Superstitions

Many people believed that on the eve of October 31st good spirits were able to communicate with the living. If we are to believe ancient folklore and legend, we can cast love spells on Halloween. Follow the instructions below to find out which lucky man could become your husband!

To see your future husband

Wait until darkness has fallen on the eve of Halloween and sit in a dark room with the lights out. Light a candle and position it in front of a mirror. Either comb your hair, or eat an apple and concentrate on your reflection. It is believed that the image of your future husband will appear in the glass, standing behind you. Make sure that you do not turn around to see him in the flesh, otherwise the image will disappear, along with your chances of marrying him!

Another way to see your future husband is to peel an apple at midnight on Halloween. You should then hang the peel on a nail by the front door. The initials of the first man to enter through the door will be the same as the initials of your husband.

To find out who will be the first to marry

Take four cups and place them on a circular table. Put a ring in one cup, a coin in another, a sprig of heather or orange blossom in the third, and leave the fourth empty. All involved should be blindfolded and each person in turn should carefully walk around the table three times. On the third and final rotation, the person should reach down and touch one of the cups. Depending on what the cup contains, this will determine that person's future marriage. The first person to touch the cup with orange blossom or heather will be the first to wed. The person who touches the cup with the coin will never want for anything. The cup with the ring denotes a lifetime of devoted love, while the empty cup means that a single life is probable.

Hallowe'en Greetings

On Hallowe'en.
By pumpkin's light, This witch
Will help you choos...

Hallowe'en

May fate reveal
By candle's gleam your own
True love on Hallowe'en.

To find out whether your love will last

Sit before an open fire with a friend at dusk on Halloween night. Each take a nut and place each at the front of the flames. If both of the nuts glow and smolder, it means that you are greatly suited to each other, and that your friendship will endure the test of time. However, if either (or even worse, both) of the nuts burst or crackle ferociously, it means that you will quarrel with each other constantly and that there will be a lack of sympathy in your friendship.

Lucky Dip

This Halloween, be prepared with a bucketful of treats for the revellers who come knocking on your door. But don't just stick to chocolate and candy. Here are some great ideas for surprising unsuspecting trick-or-treaters— why should they be the only ones to play tricks?

When the costumed mischief-makers come to your house this Halloween—whether or not they have been invited—you would be well advised to have some treats ready to hand out, if only to avoid having dastardly tricks played upon you. And if you are hosting a Halloween party, you will also need some treats to hand out as party prizes or going-home gifts.

What to do when trick-or-treaters call

✻ Prepare slips of paper, on each of which is written a funny Halloween task. Instead of playing their own tricks on you, visitors should be made to select one of the pieces of paper and perform the task before you will hand over any treats. Examples might be: "Howl like a wolf," "Sing a spooky song," "Do a Frankenstein impersonation," or "Pretend to be a rabid dog."

✻ Give away booby prizes instead of candy and money—what about a bag of sand or flour, an empty candy wrapper or the cardboard tube from a toilet paper roll?

✻ When you answer the door, act scared; run around in circles, screaming, then slam the door.

✻ Hand out a "menu" of treats you offer, and ask them to choose what they would like—then present them with a bill for what they have chosen.

Some other tricks to play

* Tie some soda cans to the rear bumper of your neighbor's car.

* Fill a margarine tub with a sticky mixture of hair gel, shaving foam, shampoo, and flour, and make your victims plunge their hands into it.

* Put a rubber snake or some plastic spiders in the mail box.

* Cut a hole in the lid of a shoe box and place something "sinister" inside. Invite people to put their hand in and guess what it is.

* Scratch at your neighbors' doors (without damaging the paintwork) and howl like a wolf.

* Coat the palm of your hand with hair gel or honey and shake hands with your victim.

* Fill a plastic bottle with something smelly—such as a mixture of vinegar, garlic, shampoo, and other ingredients. Label the bottle with a skull and crossbones and the word "poison." Keep the bottle corked until your "victim" is ready to smell it.

* Make a noise! Hit a metal pie plate with a wooden spoon, blow a trumpet, or shake a tambourine, promising to stop when you are offered a treat.

Dismembered Finger

Halloween night has arrived and you are all dressed up and ready for mischief. Now you have to decide what tricks you can play on your unsuspecting victims. This is an ultra-easy trick and you only need one prop—a matchbox. There are more tricks on page 175.

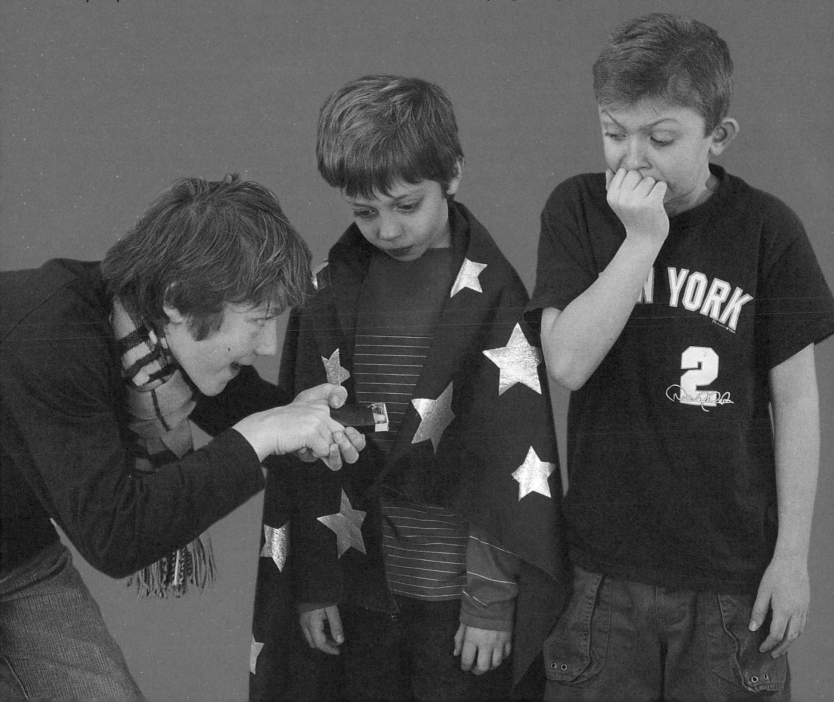

1 Cut a hole in the base of a matchbox. Make sure the hole is big enough for you to insert your finger and allow the sleeve of the box to slide back and forth.

3 Stick your finger through the hole, gripping the base with the rest of your fingers. If you like, you can drip some red paint on cotton batting around your finger, to look like blood.

2 Glue some straw in the bottom of the base.

4 Close the box—then, when you are ready, slide back the lid and wiggle your finger!

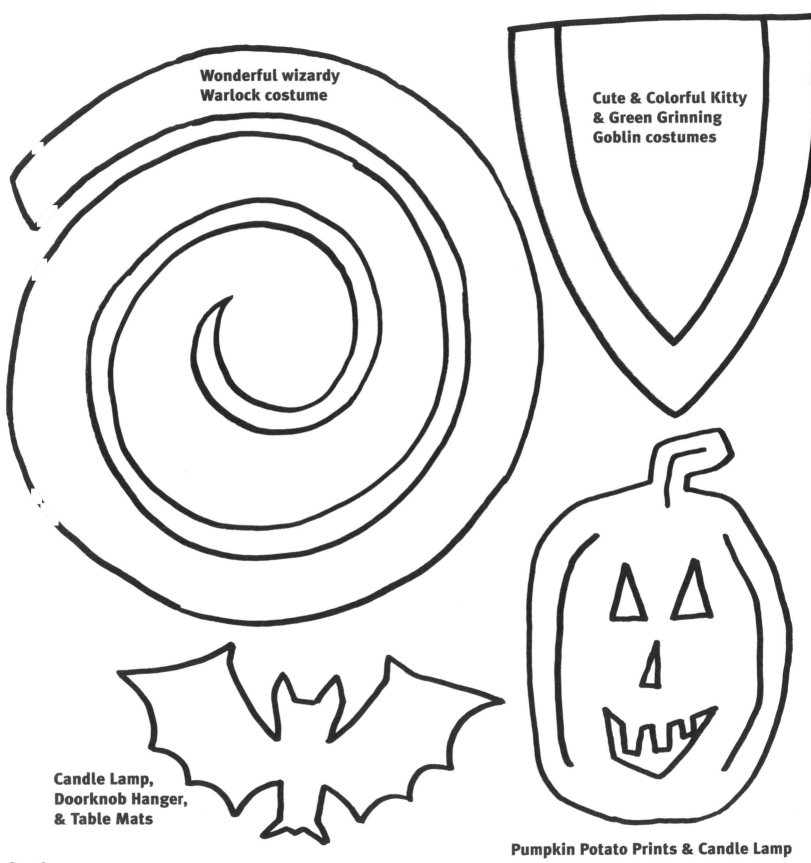

Wonderful wizardy Warlock costume

Cute & Colorful Kitty & Green Grinning Goblin costumes

Candle Lamp, Doorknob Hanger, & Table Mats

Pumpkin Potato Prints & Candle Lamp

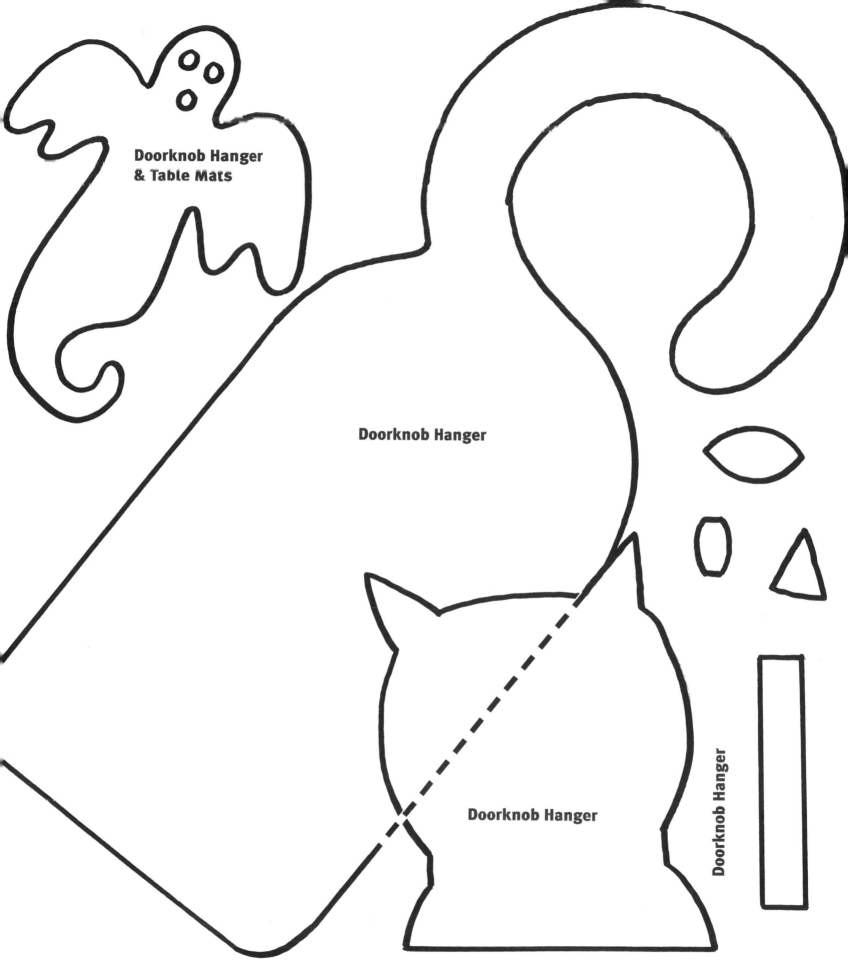

Doorknob Hanger
& Table Mats

Doorknob Hanger

Doorknob Hanger

Doorknob Hanger

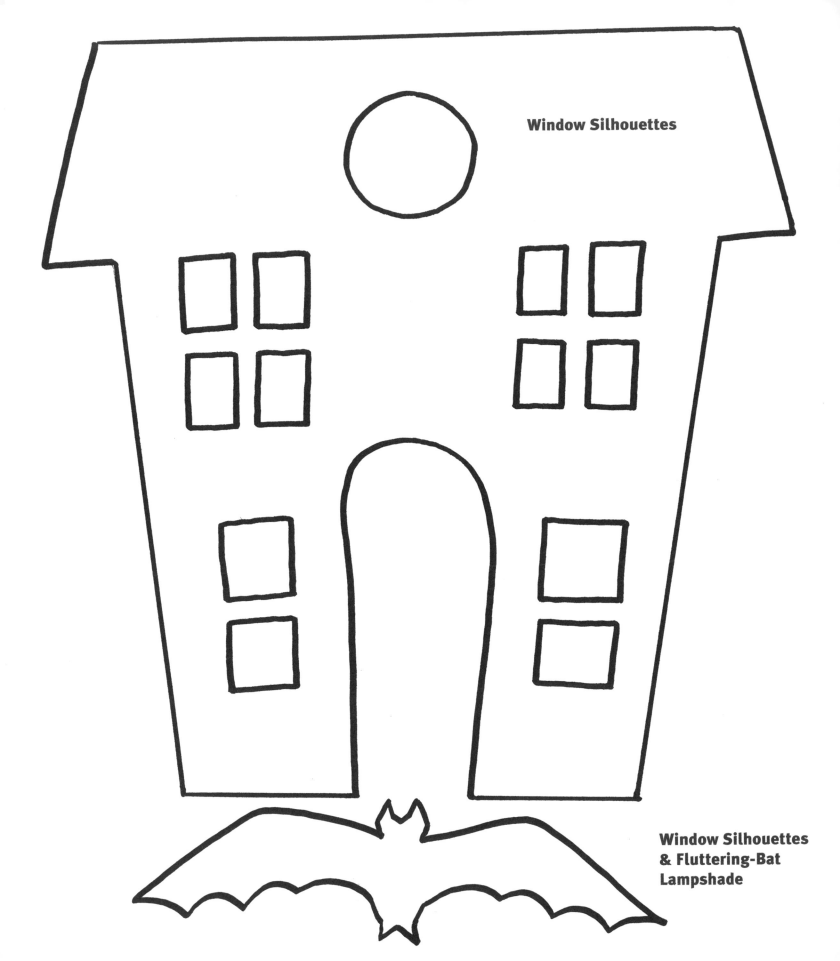

Window Silhouettes

Window Silhouettes
& Fluttering-Bat
Lampshade

Window Silhouettes

Table Mats

Halloween Bunting

Witch
finger puppet

Witch
finger puppet

Pumpkin Head
& Mummy
finger puppets

Zombie & Witch
finger puppets

Devil
finger puppet

Pumpkin Head
finger puppet

jacket for Zombie
finger puppet

Halloween Scrapbook

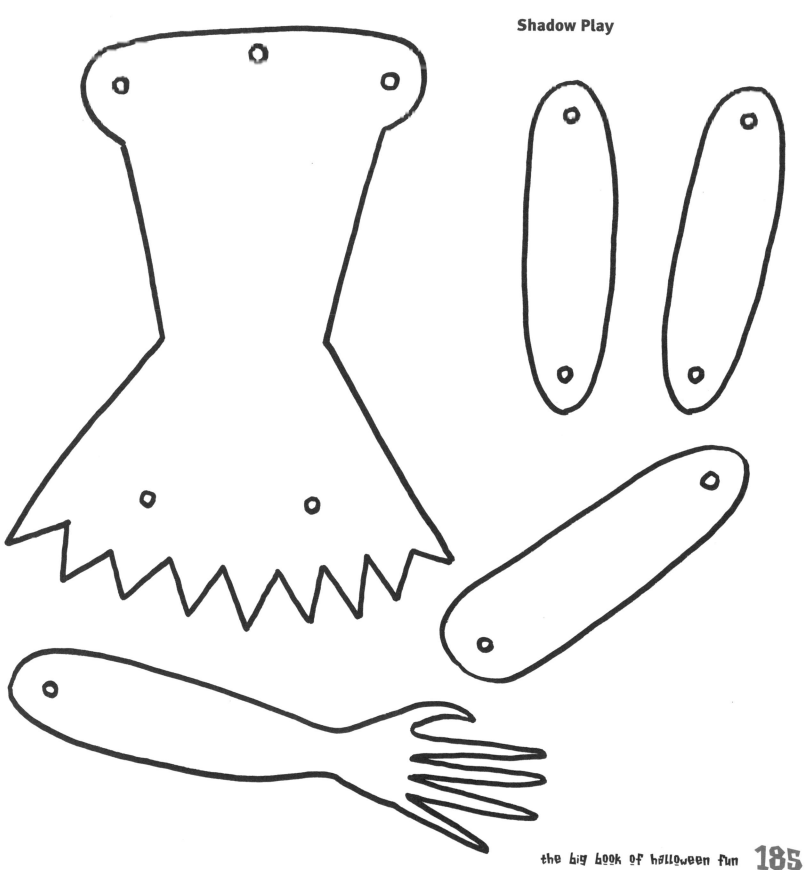

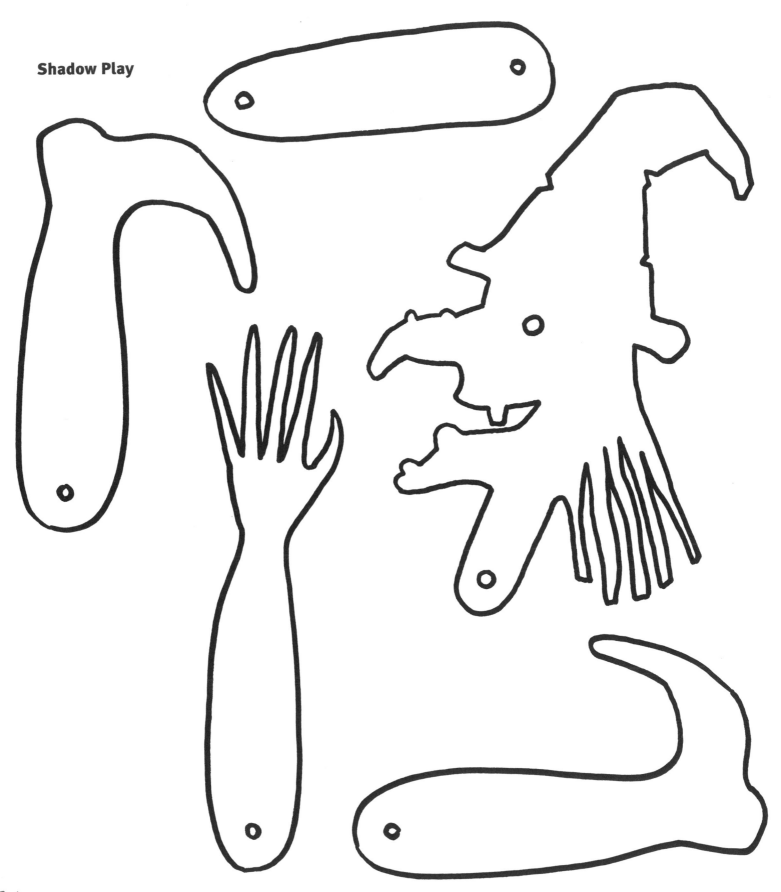

Index

Acknowledgments

MQ Publications would like to thank the following models
for their wonderful contribution to this book:

Edith Cockrell, Dirk Kalff, Sebastian Kalff, Edmund Nagle-Rose,
Luke Nicholson, Alexandra Ortolja-Baird,
Daniel Watson, Hope Wilson

Home economy: Lorna Brash

Picture Credits

p.10 © Mary Evans Picture Library; p.27 © Mary Evans Picture Library;
p.28 © SuperStock; pp.60–61 Copyright © Tecstra Systems & tecstra.com 2005;
p.64 © SuperStock; p.93 © Mary Evans Picture Library;
p.165 © SuperStock; p.173 © Mary Evans Picture Library